THEMATIC UNIT
RENAISSANCE

Written by Linda J. Larsen

Illustrated by Cheryl Buhler and Keith Vasconcelles

Teacher Created Materials, Inc.
P.O. Box 1040
Huntington Beach, CA 92647
©1994 Teacher Created Materials, Inc.
Made in U.S.A.

ISBN 1-55734-580-5

Teacher Created Materials

Table of Contents

Introduction

Renaissance contains a captivating whole language, historical thematic unit based on the years from 1300 to 1650. Its pages are filled with a wide variety of lesson ideas and reproducible pages designed for use with intermediate, middle, and junior high school students. At its core are three high-quality young adult literature selections, *The Renaissance, The High Voyage: The Final Crossing of Christopher Columbus*, and *Bard of Avon: The Story of William Shakespeare*. Also included are biographies and activities about Leonardo da Vinci and Michelangelo.

For each literature selection there are activities included which set the stage for reading, encourage enjoyment of the book, and extend the concepts. The theme is carried through with activities in the curricular areas of language arts, social studies, science, math, art, music, and life skills.

Challenging thematic units should be planned with an understanding of the reading level and organizational ability of the individual and unique group that will be participating in the unit. Some classes will take more time to cover the unit, while others will be able to do more projects independently or in cooperative learning groups.

This thematic unit includes:

+ **literature selections**—summaries of three books with related lessons that cross the curriculum

+ **planning guides**—suggestions for sequencing lessons and activities each day of the unit

+ **poetry**—suggested selections and lessons enabling students to write their own sonnets

+ **writing ideas**—writing activities across the curriculum, including making their own books

+ **curriculum connections**—in language arts, math, social studies, science, music, life skills, and art

+ **group projects**—to encourage cooperative learning

+ **culminating activities**—which require students to synthesize their learning and produce products that can be shared with others

+ **a bibliography**—suggested additional fiction and nonfiction books, computer programs, music, and teacher resources.

To keep this valuable resource intact so it can be used year after year, you may wish to punch holes in the pages and store them in a three-ring binder.

Introduction *(cont.)*

Why Whole Language?

A whole language approach involves children using all modes of communication: reading, writing, listening, observing, illustrating, experiencing, and doing. Communication skills are interconnected and integrated into lessons that emphasize the whole of language rather than isolating its parts. The lessons revolve around the selected literature. Reading is not taught as a subject separate from writing and spelling, for example. A child reads, writes, speaks, listens, etc., in response to a literature experience introduced by the teacher. In a way, language skills grow naturally, stimulated by involvement and interest in the topic at hand.

Why Thematic Planning?

One useful tool for implementing an integrated whole language program is thematic planning. By choosing a theme with correlating literature selections for a unit of study, a teacher can plan activities throughout a day to encourage a cohesive, in-depth study of the topic. Students will be practicing and applying their skills in meaningful contexts. Consequently, they will tend to learn and retain more. Both teachers and students will be freed from a day that is broken into unrelated segments of isolated drill and practice.

Why Cooperative Learning?

Along with academic skills and content, students need to learn social skills. No longer can this area of development be taken for granted. Students must learn to work cooperatively in groups in order to function well in modern society. Group activities should be a regular part of school life, and teachers should consciously include social objectives as well as academic objectives in their planning. For example, a group working together to write a play may need to select a leader. The teacher should make clear to the students the qualities of good leader-follower group interaction and monitor them just as he/she would state and monitor the academic goals of the project.

4

The Renaissance

by Tim Wood

Summary

This book is one of the See Through History series. In addition to a full complement of detailed and well-captioned illustrations, it contains four transparent overlay pages so that students can "see through" important items of the time. They can study the inside and outside of Columbus' Santa Maria, a Florentine palace, a print shop, and St. Peter's Cathedral. Two-page, easily-read-aloud sections give an overview of twenty-one Renaissance topics including city-states, the rise of trade, exploration, painting and sculpture, women at court, technology, and medical advances. Thus, the book provides a framework for a three to four week unit on the Renaissance if each section is covered in one or two days.

Below is a sample plan for teaching the Renaissance unit. Each lesson will take one or more days. Adapt the plan to fit your needs and those of your students.

Sample Plan

Lesson 1
- Read "Old Ideas" and "The Great Rebirth."
- Choose from suggested activities, page 6.

Lesson 2
- Read "City-States" and "The Art of Government."
- Choose from suggested activities, page 7.

Lesson 3
- Read "The Rise of Trade," "Exploration," and "The Ships."
- Do section on *The High Voyage*. (pages 14-28)

Lesson 4
- Read "Painting and Sculpture," "Architecture," and "Churches and Cathedrals."
- Choose from suggested activities, page 8.
- Do section on Great Renaissance Artists. (pages 43-47)

Lesson 5
- Read "Wealthy Patrons" and "Palaces and Villas."
- Choose from suggested activities, page 8.

Lesson 6
- Read "Women at Court."
- Choose from suggested activities, page 8.
- Do section on Renaissance Music and Instruments. (pages 71-72)

Lesson 7
- Read "Alchemy and Science," "Astronomy," and "Medical Advances."
- Choose from suggested activities, page 9.

Lesson 8
- Read "Technology" and "Printing."
- Choose from suggested activities, page 10.

Lesson 9 *(optional)*
- Read "Warfare."
- Choose from suggested activities, page 10.

Lesson 10 *(optional)*
- Read "The Reformation."
- Choose from suggested activities, page 10.

Lesson 11
- Read "The Spread of Ideas."
- Choose from suggested activities, page 11.
- Do Shakespeare section. (pages 29-42)

Lesson 12
- Hold a Renaissance Faire to culminate your unit. (pages 75-76.)

Overview of Activities

The following are comments, discussion topics, and activities that correspond to suggested groupings of chapters from *The Renaissance*. This particular order, which is not the exact order in which they appear in the book, seems to provide a logical sequence in which to present a Renaissance unit. Sections and pages from this thematic unit book are referred to for use within this framework. The order in which the sections are presented, however, can be altered to meet the needs of your classroom.

Setting the Stage

A unit on the Renaissance lends itself well to a focus on research skills. Taking the time to organize your classroom for such activities will pay off in better research projects. Begin by collecting as many resources about the Renaissance as possible. (See bibliography, pages 77-78 for suggestions.) Those with pictures will be especially helpful. Display these at various research centers around the room. You may wish to have a center on explorers, one on artists, one on Shakespeare, and one on the Renaissance in general. In addition, a center with art supplies will be helpful. See page 55 for directions on preparing a way to display time lines and other work created by the students.

Have students prepare a journal to be used during the unit. As a way to begin familiarizing themselves with the research materials in the room, have them peruse the displays to find a Renaissance symbol to use as the cover graphic for their journal. Suggestions for journal topics will appear throughout this book.

Enjoying the Book

"Old Ideas" and "The Great Rebirth"

To set the historical stage for your Renaissance unit, read "Old Ideas." Then have students begin work on a time line for the period. (See page 55 for suggestions.) The "Key Dates and Glossary" at the back of the book will be helpful.

Help students see that Renaissance refers to a "rebirth" or a rediscovery and continuation of the learning and creativity that had begun in classical Greece and Rome but had slowed down considerably during the Middle Ages.

Discuss the contribution of Francesco Petrarca (Petrarch) to the beginning of the Renaissance. How have books been important to the sharing of learning? Have students bring in a book to share with the class. Have them tell what they learned from the book and/or why they would include it in a permanent collection for future scholars. Then, have them develop a list of ten (or any number of your choosing) books that should be preserved for future generations. Develop lists in small groups first and then work together to reach consensus on a class list.

6

Overview of Activities *(cont.)*

"City-States" and "The Art of Government"

Note the difference between typical feudal government, as described in the "Old Ideas" section, and the Italian city-state type of government. A Venn diagram may be useful for this activity.

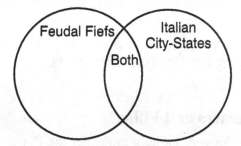

Have students follow the directions to color the map of Renaissance Italy on page 12.

Use pages 51-52 to learn about the work of everyday people during Renaissance times. Develop a list of crafts that are practiced today and may also have been practiced during the Renaissance. As a homework project, have students research and complete a craft project during the unit for display at your Renaissance Faire. Use page 53 on guild signs and have students design their own signs for the craft they are preparing.

During the Renaissance, power to govern shifted from the church to civil leaders. New philosophies of government were explored. Two men who lived at almost the same time—Machiavelli, in Italy, and Sir Thomas More, in England—developed contrasting philosophies of government which they expressed in books that have become classics. You may wish to read passages from these books to your students. List characteristics of each style of government under the book title which describes it.

The Prince	*Utopia*

Discuss which man's vision of government is most like our government today. Are there governments in the world today that resemble both styles?

"The Rise of Trade," "Exploration," and "The Ships"

The previous sections pointed out that the merchant and tradesmen of the Renaissance became rich by buying and selling goods. Many of these goods were obtained or delivered by means of ever-growing trade routes. Some of these were overland routes, but most were sea routes. These three sections describe the interaction of trade, growing wealth, improved ships and navigation techniques, and exploration.

After studying these three sections, use the materials for *The High Voyage* found on pages 14 to 28.

Overview of Activities *(cont.)*

"Painting and Sculpture," "Architecture," and "Churches and Cathedrals"

After reading and studying the illustrations in these three sections, use the materials on Michelangelo and Leonardo da Vinci found on pages 43-47. There is also an activity on St. Peter's Basilica on page 68 for students to use.

Have students work in small groups using sugar cubes and prepared frosting (for mortar) to try Brunelleschi's technique for building a dome. Have them try both single-walled and double-walled domes.

"Wealthy Patrons" and "Palaces and Villas"

Discuss the practice of patronage. How did it help to further the Renaissance? Is there a similar practice today? (scholarships, endowments, National Endowment for the Arts, art collectors, charities that sponsor galleries, museums, concert halls, etc.) Why do artists often need financial assistance? Do well-off individuals have special responsibilities to their communities?

Plan a class service project in support of a local fine arts group and/or participate in a school-site beautification project.

Share photos of some of Michelangelo's Sistine Chapel paintings. See Bibliography, pages 77-78, for books that include pictures of his work. Do the art project described on page 45 to simulate what Michelangelo endured for the sake of his art.

Have students design a floor plan or a cut-away drawing for a Renaissance villa or for their own modern dream house. Some students may wish to use cardboard and boxes to make models of their drawings.

"Women at Court"

Discuss the role of wealthy Renaissance housewives. They were often the ones who chose which artists, actors, and musicians their courts would patronize. Why were they able to have the time to do this?

Play recordings of Renaissance madrigals. (See bibliography, pages 77-78).

Notice the stringed instrument in the picture. This is a lute which can be identified by the angle of the peg box (the section of the neck that holds the tuning pegs). The lute is also mentioned in the first sentence of *The High Voyage.* Study the development of stringed instruments during the Renaissance which culminated in the unmatched work of master violin maker, Antonio Stradivari, who lived at the very end of the Renaissance.

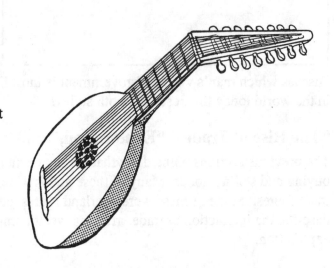

Use the music pages 71 and 72.

Also use Renaissance Women, page 13.

Overview of Activities *(cont.)*

"Alchemy and Science," "Astronomy," and "Medical Advances"

Introduce the term "alchemy" to your students. It refers to a combination of chemistry, magic, and astrology that was practiced during the Middle Ages and on into Renaissance times. Alchemists hoped to find ways to turn cheaper metals into gold and silver and to find substances that would cure any ailment and prolong human life. In addition, they sought to harmonize individuals with the universe surrounding them. Their work, strange as it may seem today, became the foundation for modern chemistry and astronomy.

To experience a chemical reaction which seems like magic, follow the directions for Mystery Matter, page 59.

Mathematics was another area that made great strides during the Renaissance. The use of symbols to show which operations should be performed was developed. To see how important these symbols are, try the activity on page 58. Students will provide the missing symbols so the number sequences make sense.

If students have not been exposed to the use of variables in basic algebra, this would be a good time to do so.

The ancient Greeks had quite accurate ideas about the Solar System, but these ideas were lost or supplanted by inaccuracies during the Middle Ages. The study of astronomy truly enjoyed a "rebirth" during the Renaissance.

The lives and ideas of Copernicus, Brahe and Kepler, Galileo, and Newton make for interesting research. Students may wish to modify the Guess Who Poster format on page 27 to present their research findings.

Discuss the oath that Galileo was forced to swear denouncing his own findings. Why would he have done this? What consequences might he have suffered if he had not? What consequences did he suffer? Does this type of repression of thought occur anywhere in the world today? Have students write a journal entry from Galileo's point-of-view regarding this incident.

Plan a trip to a planetarium if one is located in your area. At least, see if students can have an opportunity to look through a telescope. An amateur astronomer may be able to provide this.

The invention of the microscope, which allowed the discovery that germs cause diseases, led to great advances in medicine and public health. Let students have an opportunity to use a microscope to see the germs on their bodies by following the simple directions on page 59.

The uncontrollable epidemic of the Black Death or Plague also encouraged the advance of medical research. One of the most important findings was made by William Harvey, who showed that the heart pumped blood throughout the body through a system of veins and arteries. Students may wish to study the various human body systems and prepare labelled drawings of them as the Renaissance medical researchers did.

Overview of Activities *(cont.)*

"Technology" and "Printing"

Discuss the term technology or applied science. It is the set of "tools, machines, techniques, and processes used to produce goods and services and satisfy human needs." *(The World Book Dictionary)* During the Renaissance, scientists and inventors made great strides in applying math and science to the production of tools and machines to improve lives. From these sections, list all the items we continue to use today that were invented during the Renaissance. Have pairs or small groups of students choose an item from the list and research the history of its development. An effective way for students to present their findings would be a pictorial time line as shown in this sample. (See page 55 for additional time line suggestions.)

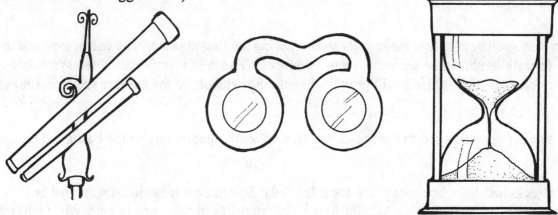

Study the section on printing, being sure to notice such details as the power source for the printing plant, the types of materials used for pages and covers, and materials used to make the type.

Set up side-by-side simulations to show how the implementation of technology changes such variables as the role of the worker and the speed of the job. See page 65 for directions for the simulations.

Local newspapers or printers will often let students visit their printing plants. Such a field trip would be invaluable to help students see the technological advances that have occurred since books were copied by hand.

"Warfare" and "The Reformation" *(optional)*

Discuss how Renaissance technology changed the nature of war. What were people of the times warring about? What elements of modern warfare had their roots in the Renaissance?(e.g., easily moveable cannon evolved into tanks)

Students who are interested may wish to create a time line and map of the wars that were conducted during the period of the Renaissance. They may also wish to collect pictures or make models of weapons and fortifications of the time.

The rebellion against the established church which occurred during the Renaissance led to religious wars, which is why these two seemingly different sections have a loose connection. Discuss how Renaissance scholarship and technological improvements contributed to the Reformation. Compare the influence of religion in the lives of people during the Renaissance with religion in the lives of people today. Between what factions are there religious wars in the world today? Is there a conflict between religious belief and the practice of war?

10

Overview of Activities *(cont.)*

"The Spread of Ideas"

Discuss the reasons for the Renaissance spreading from Italy to the rest of Europe. Why is the Renaissance still so important today?

Examine the drawing of London's Globe Theater. Modern theater really began in such venues as this, and the classic plays of William Shakespeare were performed there. Use the section on William Shakespeare, pages 29-42.

The unit focuses on Europe from about 1300 to 1650; however, changes were occurring all over the world during this time period. A good book describing these changes is *Exploration and Discovery From AD 1450 to AD 1750* (Usborne Picture World History) by Dr. Anne Millard. (See Bibliography for ordering information.) Full of illustrations, this book is a wonderful supplement to the materials presented in *The Renaissance* by Tim Wood. Moreover, it also contains information about The Incas in South America, the Turks and the Persians, Russia, European settlers in North America, Africa, India, China, and Japan. Not only will students enjoy and learn from the many pictures in this book, but they also will gain a better sense of history when they see that settlement of North America, for example, began near the end of the European Renaissance and the Inca empire was established and then destroyed within the time period. This book also contains several lists of key dates which will help students develop time lines. (See page 55 for time line activity suggestions.)

Another excellent text and picture resource for this unit is *The Renaissance and the New World* (History of Everyday Things series) by Giovanni Caselli. (See bibliography, page 77.) Students will get a real sense of everyday life in several parts of Europe during the Renaissance. In addition, New World settlements of the 1700's are included.

Extending the Book

Culminating Activity

Conclude the unit with a Renaissance Faire to celebrate and display the learning which has taken place. Suggestions for planning and conducting this activity may be found on pages 75 and 76.

Come join us at the faire

Renaissance Italy

Around 1400, present-day Italy was made up of many small and large city-states. Each had its own government. Many of the laws were based on the "class" people belonged to, not on equal rights. Some states were ruled by foreign countries. In other states, rich families controlled the government. Many of these families gained their wealth through trading. Italian traders would buy goods cheaply in one country and sell them for a higher price somewhere else. This trading helped to spread the new ideas and inventions of the Renaissance around the world.

The wealth of these families made it possible for them to have the leisure time to become educated and to value the fine arts. They became patrons of scholars and other talented people. For example, the famous family which ruled Florence was the Medici (MED a chee) family. They paid artists like Michelangelo to paint pictures and build churches to beautify their city.

Directions: Use red to color the city-state ruled by the Medici family. Then use other colors to color the rest of the city-states so that no adjoining states are the same color. Add a compass rose showing north, south, east, and west. Compare your map with a map of modern Italy. List the cities which can be found on both maps.

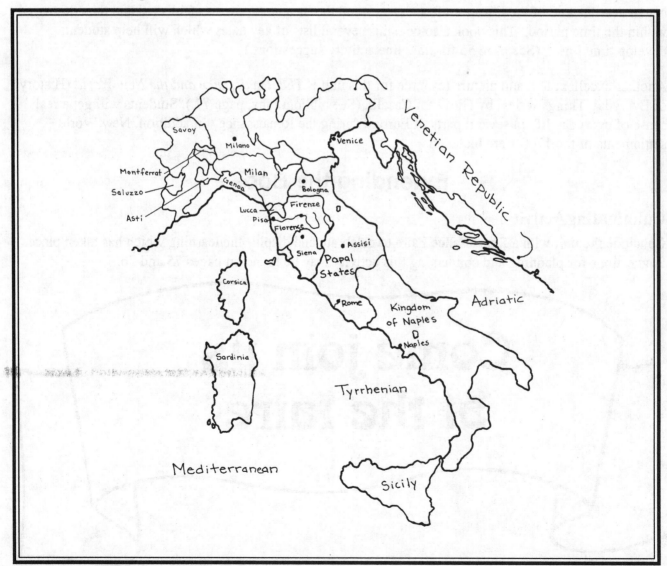

Renaissance Women

During the Renaissance most of the information was written by men about men. But there were some very influential women from these times. Choose one of the women who lived during the Renaissance from the list below and follow the steps to complete a research assignment.

Joan of Arc (France) 1412-1431
Queen Isabella (Spain) 1451-1504
Mary Tudor or Mary I (England) 1516-1558
Catherine de Medici (France) 1519-1589
Elizabeth I (England) 1533-1603
Mary Stuart (Scotland) 1542-1587
Artemisia Gentileschi (Italy) 1593-1652

Directions:

1. Find resource books and take notes. Make sure you include the following information:
   - Your sources of information (a list of all the books you used)
   - A list of important dates and events
   - Her accomplishments and contributions
   - When and where she was born and died
   - Influential people in her life
   - Unusual facts about her life
   - Her contribution to history

2. Next, rewrite your information into an interesting report. Add visuals to enhance your work. For example:
   - A map showing where important events in her life happened
   - Pictures illustrating the interesting parts of her life
   - A drawing of what she looked like, or the type of clothing she would have worn
   - A picture time line of the main events
   - A collage poster of her life
   - A museum display for the school library that represents her accomplishments
   - A 3-D model about a special place in her life
   - A mobile showing pictures and events in her life

3. Present your report to your class. You may wish to use one of the following to make your presentation especially interesting.
   - Dress as the character and read your report aloud to your class.
   - Perform a play for the class about her life.
   - Write a script for a mock interview with your character. Have a friend help you conduct the interview for your class.
   - Use your imagination about other ways you can share your information.

The High Voyage: The Final Crossing of Christopher Columbus

by Olga Litowinsky

Summary

In 1502, Fernando Columbus sailed across the Ocean Sea with his father, Christopher Columbus. It was Fernando's first sea voyage, and his father's fourth trip to the Indies. This action-packed story tells of friendship, adventure, and courage. Fernando experiences first-hand the marvels of the New World and the dangers of hurricanes, mutiny, and being stranded. It shows us a new dimension of the Columbus legend and the Spanish conquest.

Note: This book tells a wonderful story but contains a realistic view of the Spanish oppression towards the natives they encounter. It also has many references towards religion. There are also some very graphic descriptions of practices (e.g., cannibalism at the end of Chapter VII) that you will need to be aware of. As a teacher, you will want to pre-read this book before introducing it to your class.

This outline is a suggested plan for using the various activities that are presented in this book. You should adapt these ideas to fit your own classroom situation and the ability level of your students.

Sample Plan

Lesson 1
- Introduce the four voyages of Columbus 1492-1502.
- Setting the Stage activities, page 15.
- Make banners, page 28.

Lesson 2
- Continue Setting the Stage activities.
- Use The Age of Exploration, page 26.
- Begin research for Guess Who posters, page 27.
- Introduce vocabulary words for Section 1. (See Enjoying the Book #2, page 16, and page 19.)

Lesson 3
- Begin reading *The High Voyage*, Prologue and Chapters I - IV.
- Add new information to classroom diary. (See Enjoying the Book #1)
- Use discussion/journal questions for section. (page 20)
- Introduce vocabulary words for Section 2. (page 19)
- Put together Guess Who posters, and add first clue.
- Label caravel, page 25.

Lesson 4
- Read Chapters V - IX.
- Add new information to classroom diary.
- Use discussion/journal questions for section. (page 20)
- Introduce vocabulary words for Section 3. (page 19)
- Add second clue to Guess Who posters.

Lesson 5
- Read Chapters X - XIII.
- Add new information to classroom diary.
- Use discussion/journal questions for section. (page 20)
- Introduce vocabulary words for Section 4. (page 19)
- Add third clue to Guess Who posters.
- Choose an Enjoying the Book activity to do in a group or individually. (pages 16 and 17)

Sample Plan (cont.)

Lesson 6
- Read Chapters XIV -XVI.
- Add new information to classroom diary.
- Introduce vocabulary words for Section 5. (page 19)
- Use discussion/journal questions for section. (page 20)
- Add fourth clue to Guess Who posters.
- Continue working on Enjoying the Book activity.

Lesson 7
- Read Chapters XVII - XX.
- Add new information to classroom diary.
- Introduce vocabulary words for Section 6. (page 19)
- Use discussion/journal questions for section. (page 20)
- Add fifth clue to Guess Who posters.

- Finish working on Enjoying the Book activity.
- Use Mathematics in the Caribbean. (page 22)

Lesson 8
- Finish reading the book, Chapters XXI - XXVI, Epilogue, and Author's Note.
- Complete last entries for the diary.
- Use discussion/journal questions for section. (page 20)
- Add sixth clue to Guess Who posters.

Lesson 9
- Use Sequencing and Summary. (page 21)
- Add last clue to Guess Who posters.
- Choose from Extending the Book activities, page 17.

Lesson 10
- Reveal answers to Guess Who posters.
- Completion of all activities and class presentations.

Overview of Activities
Setting the Stage

1. Prepare the classroom with a bulletin board for art and writing projects, a table with resource books from the library, butcher paper for word lists, murals, and classroom "diary," and a string across the room for time lines, mobiles, and banners.

2. Duplicate the maps on pages 23-24 for each student and enlarge them using an overhead projector for wall-mounted models. As the caravels travel from one place to another, label the stops on the wall maps and mark the route. Have students label the stops on their own maps which will be kept in their journals.

3. In their journals have students write a paragraph including information they already know about Christopher Columbus. At the end of the book, have them write another paragraph adding any new information. Compare the results.

4. Have the students brainstorm about some other explorers they are familiar with from this era (1400 through 1600). Use an overhead projector to show a map of the world and trace their routes.

5. A caravel is the type of ship Columbus used on this voyage. Find some pictures and information about this ship (see "The Ships" section of *The Renaissance* by Tim Wood, for example) and other forms of transportation used during the Age of Exploration. Make a collage of drawings and pictures showing transportation before and after the Renaissance. Use page 25 to further study caravels.

Overview of Activities (cont.)

Enjoying the Book

1. Keep a class "diary" as you read the story. Put up one piece of butcher paper for each of the following categories: Places, Animal Life, Foods, Events, People. As you complete each reading section, have the class suggest new things to add to each page. Use these lists for research topics.

2. Use the vocabulary word lists as you read each section. Choose the amount from each list that is appropriate for your class. Write the chosen words on a large piece of butcher paper. Introduce them before reading each section. Discuss what they mean and write down their definitions. Encourage the students to use these words in their writing activities. Additional suggestions for using the vocabulary words can be found on page 18.

3. In Chapter IV, using a compass was very important to the navigation of the ships. Bring some directional compasses to class. Have the students, in small groups, "navigate" their way across the playground to a special destination of their choice. Have them record their routes in terms of number of steps and compass directions. For example, from the water fountain take 2 steps north, then take 5 steps south-east, etc. Trade routes with other groups and see if they navigate the routes correctly. Discuss the problems of navigating this way and how it affected the explorers of Columbus's time.

4. After reading Chapter V, enjoy a snack of as many of the shipboard foods listed as possible. Do students agree that the sailors were "eating well"?

5. Create a mural of the four caravels and the events that occur as they sail across the Ocean Sea.

6. Make a picture time line of the story. (See page 55.) Add a new picture for each reading section.

7. Use toothpicks, craft sticks, and/or other art materials to build replicas of caravels or other forms of transportation used during the Age of Exploration.

8. Write a letter from the point-of-view of one of the characters, telling of the events and places you have seen. Example: You could be Paco writing to his sister Caridad, Fernando to his Uncle Diego, or Columbus to Queen Isabella.

9. Often during the story, Columbus must stop for provisions or supplies. Plan a six week sailing adventure in the 1500's throughout the Caribbean for a group of ten people. Display all your information on a poster. Include the following:

    A. A map showing your route

    B. A picture of your ship showing where everything and everyone would fit

    C. A list of who is on your ship, their jobs, and the provisions on board

    D. A diary of when and where you travel, events that happen, etc.

10. While stranded on Jamaica in Chapter XXI, Fernando and Paco collect sea shells. Have students or guests bring in a shell collection to share.

Overview of Activities (cont.)

Enjoying the Book (cont.)

11. Write a five-line poem about the story using the frame below.

   Example: *noun*
   > *two adjectives*
   > *three verbs*
   > *a thought about the noun*
   > *a synonym for the noun*

Extending the Book

1. Have the students work in groups to create a "quiz" for the book. Exchange the finished quizzes with other groups to complete.

2. Make a list of three major problems from the story. Describe how they were solved and how each contributed to the story. Create a new problem that was not in the book. How would you have the characters solve it, and how would it affect the outcome of the book? Share your new problems with the class.

3. Choose a section from the story. Make a cartoon strip showing the events. Put all the cartoons together in sequence and publish a comic book version of the story.

4. Create a "What's My Line?" game using characters from the story. Have each student secretly choose a character from the story and become familiar with the job of that character as described in the book. Students will have ten chances to ask yes/no questions regarding the job of the character. If the job is identified before ten questions are asked, they can go on to guess the character. If ten questions are asked and the job has not been guessed, the person must reveal his secret identity and then give the class a final chance to guess the line of work.

5. Make a travel poster for one or more of the places Fernando visited.

6. Choose a section from the book and act it out as a play. Perform it for your class or for a younger group.

7. Make a time line of all of Columbus' four voyages or Queen Isabella's life. Use Time Lines on page 55 for directions.

Suggestions for Using the Vocabulary Lists

1. Use the words as spelling lists.

2. Find the vocabulary word within the book. Copy down the sentence it was in. Rewrite the sentence using a synonym in place of the vocabulary word or write your own sentence using the word the same way as the author.

3. Make word puzzles. Give students pieces of graph paper to make their own word searches or crossword puzzles. Exchange with others in the class or another group to complete.

4. Divide the class into groups. Each group is responsible for creating a game using their word list. The class can then play each group's game. Examples: Bingo, Wheel of Fortune, Jeopardy, Concentration, Spelling Bee, etc.

5. Categorize the words into groups. Example: nouns, verbs, adjectives, adverbs, etc.

6. Alphabetize each list of words.

7. Using newspaper headlines, cut out letters to form the words from the list. See how many the students can make in twenty minutes. Or, see how many of the complete words you can find being used in newspapers and magazines. Make a class collage of the words they find.

8. Use the words to write sentences, stories, or poems.

9. Practice keyboarding skills on a computer or typewriter using the word lists.

10. Create word scrambles. Exchange with a friend or group to solve.

Vocabulary Lists for
The High Voyage

Section 1 *(Chapters I - IV)*

venture	scroll	omen	sedately	fortress
competence	caravels	armada	quell	grommet
nuisance	navigator	lute	fluttering	hoisted
squall	rival	scoundrels	mystified	inverted

Section 2 *(Chapters V - IX)*

prosperous	quip	hindrance	siesta	rummaged
trifles	confidant	harpooned	surveyed	thatch
lulled	aristocratic	leagues	frond	pacified
brisk	bridled	etched	inhabitants	refuge

Section 3 *(Chapters X - XIII)*

sullen	awe	surged	currents	precious
strait	enthralled	tattooed	continuous	lamented
clambered	scribe	interior	embalmed	ransom
tempest	ordeal	manatee	gesticulating	flint
elaborate	impediment	festivity	tedious	consoled
pendant	shunned	screeching	effigy	spectacle

Section 4 *(Chapters XIV - XVI)*

inlet	province	pursue	souvenir	bartered
accurate	reciting	gruel	denounce	pitiable
arc	isthmus	stucco	provisions	gully
placate	caulked	feuds	turquoise	terrain

Section 5 *(Chapters XVII - XX)*

suspicious	confidence	negotiate	coronets	commotion
toppling	seized	mutiny	toil	marooned
ironic	sallow	massacred	booty	hulk
delirious	venture	rampart	sieve	fortified

Section 6 *(Chapter XXI - Epilogue)*

particular	laboriously	traitors	elated	scoffed
navigator	futile	pardon	cauterize	embarked
ingenuity	tutelage	glimpse	mutiny	sequestered
eclipses	lamentations	conspiracy	phantom	rebellions

Discussion or Journal Questions for *The High Voyage*

Section 1 *(Prologue and Chapters I - IV)*

1. Why is Christopher Columbus going on a fourth voyage? When and where does the story start? Describe the main character. From whose point-of-view is the story told? What misgivings about the trip does the main character feel?
2. Name the four ships that start on this journey. Which one do Fernando and Paco travel on? Explain how a compass works. Why is it important to the navigator? What is a "watch"? How long does a watch last? Why are watches necessary? Explain Paco's job.

Section 2 *(Chapters V - IX)*

1. Describe shipboard life as portrayed in these chapters. Add to this description as you read the rest of the book. What kinds of foods are eaten on board the ship? What kinds of foods did Fernando and the other sailors miss from home?
2. What is a "cooper"? Why is his job important on the ship?
3. What were some of the fears of the sailors? Collect examples of these throughout the book. Which fears are justified?
4. Why was Paco so unhappy?
5. Compare the personalities and lives of Fernando and Paco. How are they alike and different?
6. Why does Columbus decide to land at Santo Domingo in spite of the Queen's request? What happens when he tries to do so?

Section 3 *(Chapters X - XIII)*

1. Describe the storm and its results.
2. Christopher Columbus and Fernando both feel they are treating the natives properly. What do you feel? Collect evidence from this section and the following ones to support your opinion.
3. What words from Fernando's father made him feel so good? Why did he feel this way?

Section 4 *(Chapters XIV - XVI)*

1. Where does Columbus think he is? Where is he actually? Why does he make this error?
2. What decision does Columbus make about the fate of the expedition? Why?

Section 5 *(Chapters XVII - XX)*

1. Why does Columbus think it necessary to capture the Quibian? What happens when he tries? What is your opinion of this tactic?
2. How many ships sail back to Spain? Why?
3. At the end of Chapter XIX, Columbus and his ships are marooned. Before reading the rest of the book, predict how Columbus will solve this problem.

Section 6 *(Chapters XXI - Epilogue and Author's Note)*

1. How long are the ships marooned? Paco thinks staying on Jamaica might not be so bad. Why?
2. What is a mutiny? Describe the one that occurs in this section.
3. Describe the events surrounding the eclipse of the moon. Was Columbus right in using this natural phenomena the way he did?
4. What is your opinion of Paco's decision?
5. When and where did the story finish? How have we come to know this story?

Sequencing and Summary Mobiles

Identifying important events and placing them in order are essential comprehension skills. Use this activity with *The High Voyage* or other reading materials to develop and reinforce these skills.

Summary Mobiles

1. Divide the text into appropriate sections for your students' level. The sections for *The High Voyage* as identified in the Sample Lesson Plans (pages 14-15) may be used. Divide the class into the same number of groups. (This may also be done as an individual project.)

2. In their groups, have students identify and discuss the following items for inclusion on their mobile.
   - Title and Author of Book
   - Section of Book Being Studied
   - Setting (Time and Place) of Section (may be more than one)
   - Major Characters
   - Important Events

   You may wish to add more structure to the activity by designating a specific number of characters and events for students to identify.

3. Each group will need the following supplies:
   - wire coat hanger
   - drawing paper
   - scissors
   - tape or glue
   - coloring materials
   - thread or string
   - hole punch

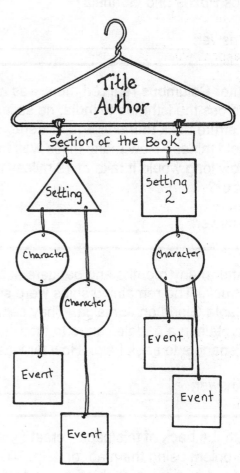

4. Using the diagram as a model, students should begin their mobiles. One side of each addition should contain a picture and the other side words. Have them arrange the additions to the mobile in a way that shows the sequence of events within their section of the story.

5. After the mobiles have been completed, each group should choose a spokesperson. In correct sequence, the groups will share and then hang their mobiles.

Mathematics in the Caribbean

Students can practice their math skills on the following word problems. Use the map of the Caribbean, page 23, or the one at the front of *The High Voyage* to help you solve these travel problems.

Problem	*Work Space*
1. One of the caravels' first stops in the Caribbean was Matinino. It took them three weeks to get there from the Canaries. If the caravels traveled at 12 miles (19.2 km) per hour, what distance did they travel? Answer: _____	
2. After surviving the hurricane outside of Santo Domingo, the voyage was underway again. They passed the islands of Los Pozos and sailed to Guanaja. About how many miles is it between Los Pozos and Guanaja? Answer: _____	
3. After Columbus realized there was no passage across the isthmus to India, he sailed from Retrete back to the village of Veragua to look for gold mines. How many miles was this trip, and how long would it take at 12 miles (19.2 km) per hour? Answer: _____	
4. After many months and dangers at sea, tragedy struck. The remaining ships were stranded at Santa Gloria on Jamaica. They sent the ship's captain in a paddle canoe to the island of Espanola to seek help. How far was this trip? Answer: _____	
5. On the back of this paper, create your own word problem using the map for help. Trade with a friend and solve each other's problems.	

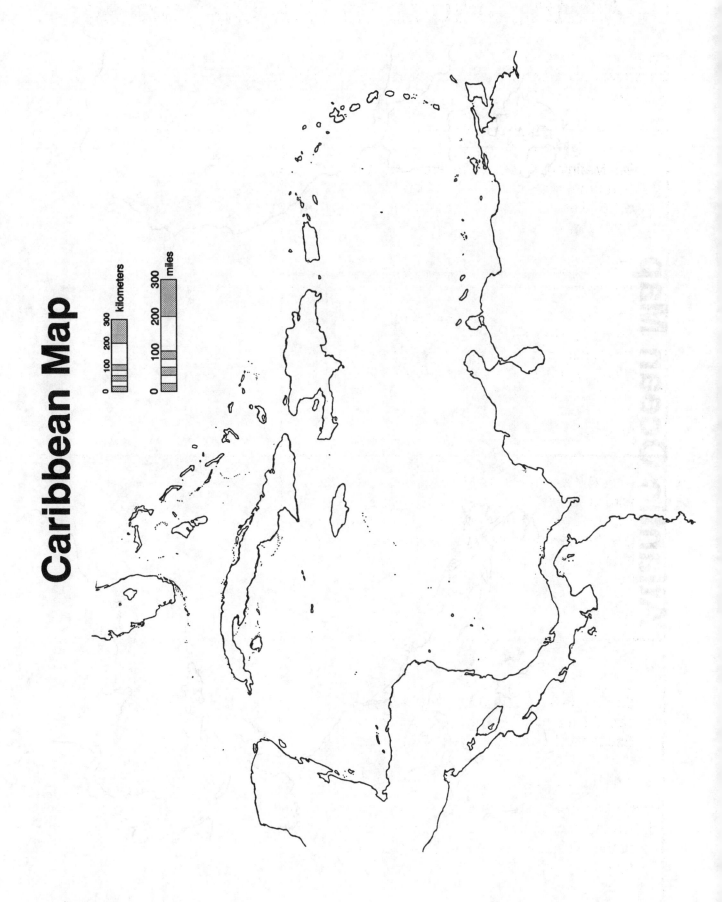

Caribbean Map

kilometers

0 100 200 300

miles

0 100 200 300

Atlantic Ocean Map

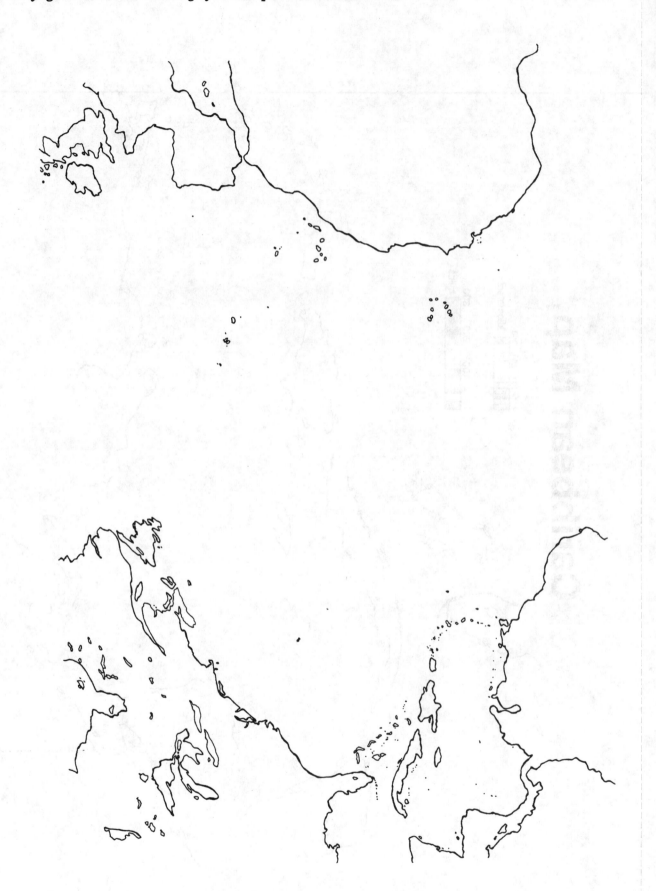

Caravels

At the beginning of the Age of Exploration, sailors needed a ship that would last on longer journeys. Using the Arab *dhow* as a model, the caravel was designed by the Portuguese. This is the type of ship used in the book *The High Voyage*. The ship weighed between 57 and 200 tons (57-200 tonnes) and could travel about 12 miles (19 km) an hour. The large, square sail on the foremast enabled it to travel favorably in the winds. It held a crew of about 40 men who lived a simple, but adventuresome and dangerous, life on board. Many sailors did not survive the long trips. As new designs were developed, the caravel became too slow and was outdated by the 16th century.

Use the word bank below and a dictionary or other reference material (including the overlay ship in *The Renaissance* by Tim Wood) to identify the parts of the caravel.

Word Bank

crow's nest	rudder	hull	mainmast	mizzenmast
foremast	forecastle	mainsail	mizzensail	foresail

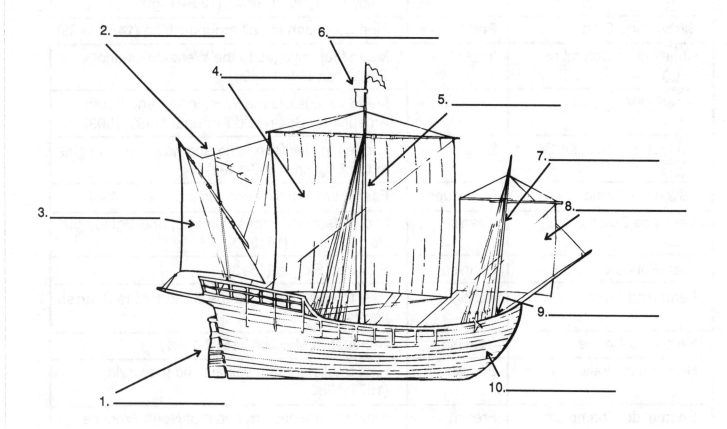

2. _____   6. _____

4. _____   5. _____

7. _____

3. _____   8. _____

9. _____

1. _____   10. _____

The Age of Exploration

The 14th, 15th, and 16th centuries are considered the greatest periods of European overseas exploration. Thanks to their predecessors—the Vikings, the Crusaders, Marco Polo, the Arabs, and the Chinese development of the compass—European explorers were able to make great strides.

The Renaissance brought on a tremendous feeling for movement and curiosity about other lands and peoples. Countries became very competitive for the rich markets of foreign lands, searching for gold, silver, and spices. The increase in commerce and business made it possible for rich merchants to increase their wealth by supporting overseas explorations. Religious leaders sought new lands to spread the ideas of Christianity. Seamen risked their lives for the love of adventure and curiosity about new ideas. Even today, this sense of adventure still exists.

Use the list of Renaissance era explorers below to help complete the activity on page 27.

Explorer	Nationality	Achievements and Dates
Leif Ericson	Norse	Probably the first European to reach mainland North America (1000?)
Marco Polo	Italian	Far-reaching journeys into Asia (1271-1295)
Prince Henry	Portuguese	Improved methods of navigation; organized many voyages to Africa (1394-1460)
Bartolomeu Dias	Portuguese	First European to sail around Africa (1487-1488)
Christopher Columbus	Italian	Made four voyages to the West Indies and Caribbean (1492-1504)
Amerigo Vespucci	Italian	Made voyages to the West indies and South America for Spain and Portugal (1497-1503)
John and Sebastian Cabot	Italian	Landed in Newfoundland and gave fishing rights to the English (1497-1498)
Vasco Da Gama	Portuguese	First European to reach India by sea (1498)
Vasco de Balboa	Spanish	Led expedition across Panama, and sighted the Pacific Ocean (1513)
Juan Ponce de Leon	Spanish	Explored Florida (1513)
Ferdinand Magellan	Portuguese	First to voyage around the world for the Spanish flag (1529-1521)
Hernando Cortes	Spanish	Conquered Mexico (1519-1521)
Sir Francis Drake	English	First Englishman to sail around the world (1577-1580)
Samuel de Champlain	French	Explored the eastern coast of North America (1603-1616)
Henry Hudson	English	Explored Hudson Bay (1609-1611)

Guess Who Poster

This project can be done by individuals or groups.

Object:

To create a cumulative poster about an explorer and see if the other students in your class can guess who it is.

Directions:

1. Choose an explorer to research. (Use the list on page 26 for ideas.)

2. You will need to find the following information:
   • ten interesting facts about his life or journeys
   • the flag of his country
   • a map showing his travels
   • the types of transportation he used

3. On poster board, put together the above information. Remember do not use his name anywhere.

4. Each day, add new information to your poster. Remember to start with less well known information first. See how many days you can keep your classmates guessing.

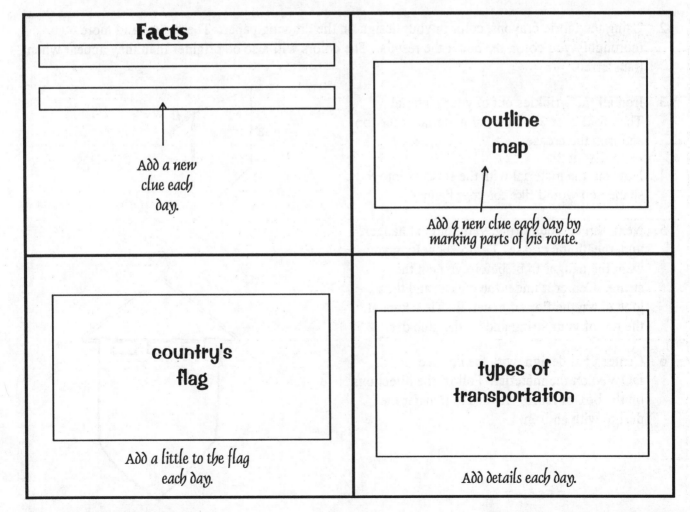

Making a Banner

Columbus' ship sailed with banners that were representational. During the Renaissance banners or flags represented families. Following the directions below, make a banner that represents you.

Display the finished banners around the classroom. Can you guess who is who?

Materials:

- a 9" x 14" (23cm x 36cm) piece of white cotton material, possibly from an old sheet
- fabric crayons (available at craft stores)
- iron
- scissors
- string, yarn, or coat hanger
- 9" x 12" (23cm x 30cm) white drawing paper
- pencil
- glue

Directions:

1. On the white drawing paper, draw a design in pencil. It should represent yourself, things you like, favorite colors, family, hobbies, etc. Do not use words, since the picture will be reversed when it is ironed onto the banner.

2. Using the fabric crayons, color in your design on the drawing paper. The darker and more thoroughly you color, the better the results. The colors will also be brighter than they appear when transferred.

3. Iron all the wrinkles out of your material. Then fold over 2" (5 cm) of material at the top and iron the crease.

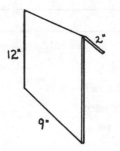

4. Now cut the material with the scissors into the shape you would like for your banner.

5. Next, thread your string, yarn, or coat hanger underneath the crease. Decide how long you want the hanger to be before you cut the string. Center it under the crease, and then glue down the flap of material. Tie a knot at the top of your string and let the glue dry.

6. Center your design, with the colored side DOWN, on the material. Follow the directions on the box of fabric crayons to transfer the design with an iron.

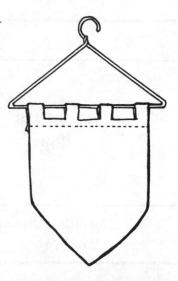

28

Bard of Avon: The Story of William Shakespeare

by Diane Stanley and Peter Vennema

Summary

The husband-wife team of Stanley and Vennema collaborated to research, write, and illustrate this picture biography of William Shakespeare. They have included up-to-date information about the poet, and their text sheds light on the ways historians reconstruct a person's life by using original source documents. You will want to share the Authors' Note at the front of the book which speaks about this type of research.

Readers of this delightful book will learn about Shakespeare's life, his plays, and the theater of the times through word and picture. In addition, they will gain an insightful glimpse into the daily lives of the people in Renaissance England.

The plan below is offered as an example of the way this book may be used. It should be adapted to meet the needs of your classroom.

Sample Plan

Lesson 1
- Pre-assess students' knowledge of Shakespeare.
- Assign Shakespearean surveys as homework. (pages 32-33)

Lesson 2
- Present the book, *The Bard of Avon.* (page 30)
- Complete Scrambled Shakespeare. (page 34)
- Listen to Shakespeare recordings or watch videos.

Lesson 3
- Review *The Bard of Avon* by making a class Big Book. (page 34)
- Write a resume for William Shakespeare. (page 35)
- Do some career exploration.
- Listen to Shakespeare recordings or read some sonnets. (page 37)
- Choose and complete an activity related to sonnets. (page 31)
- Begin choosing oral readings and practicing them. (page 39)

Lesson 4
- Find out about costumes of the Elizabethan age.
- Share information about the Old Globe Theater. (page 38)
- Do a simulation of the Old Globe's audience. (page 31)
- Present oral readings of Shakespeare's work.
- Take a field trip to see a play by Shakespeare performed.

Overview of Activities

Setting the Stage

1. "The Truth Will Out..." In order to pre-assess student's knowledge of Shakespeare and the time he lived, brainstorm as a group what student's knowledge base is and what students would like to find out. The chart can be transferred to the chalkboard, a large piece of paper, overhead transparency or copied for cooperative groups. The left side should say "What We Know" and the right side "What We Want to Discover." As you read the book, the left side information will be confirmed and the right side questions answered.

Topic: Shakespeare	
What We Know	**What We Want to Discover**

2. There are two different surveys for students to conduct before the study of the *Bard of Avon* begins. The Shakespeare Survey on page 32 has students survey family and friends to see if they have knowledge about Shakespeare. Have students conduct the survey, and then graph the results in class.

3. The second, Survey of Sayings by Shakespeare (page 33), can be done at the same time as the Shakespeare Survey or separately. After the surveys are complete, discuss what the sayings mean or assign them as journal topics.

Enjoying the Book

1. There are several ways to introduce the *Bard of Avon*. Students can read the book themselves, small groups may read it to each other, or you may opt to read it to the class. If you read it out loud, plan to read it over a few days, allowing ample time to share the illustrations. Point out the richness of the detail in the art. Ask students what they can infer about the times by looking at the pictures.

2. Complete the Scrambled Shakespeare activity on page 34. Students can do this sequencing independently or in small groups.

   A fun way to do this in groups is to make a copy for each group, cut it apart and put it in an envelope. Give each group an envelope. At a signal, students work together to put the strips in order. The first group to correctly sequence the story is the winner.

3. It is important that students hear the language of Shakespeare. Show movies or videos of Shakespearean plays. Several are available. Recordings are also available for classroom use. Since the quality and the appropriateness for the classroom of these vary, be sure to preview them before sharing with your class.

4. Bring William Shakespeare's life into the present by having students complete his resumé on page 35. Use the information from the book to complete this activity. After completing it, brainstorm a list of current day careers that Shakespeare might be interested in exploring further.

Overview of Activities (cont.)

Enjoying the Book (cont.)

5. Using the information about how sonnets are composed and Shakespeare's sonnets (pages 36-37), try some of the following activities with your students.

   - Using the rhyme pattern, have students write sonnets.
   - Everyone interprets poems differently. Have a class or group discussion about what Shakespeare was trying to express.
   - Find ten unusual words from the poem and look them up in a thesaurus for synonyms. Rewrite the poem using the new words. How does it change the poem?
   - Shakespeare uses many descriptive words in his poetry. Create a picture or drawing that creates the same mood as the poem.

6. Read the information about the Old Globe Theater on page 38. Then use it to create a simulation. Assign a group in the class to pretend to be the audience at the Old Globe. As students read and perform various scenes from Shakespeare (pages 39-40), have this group simulate the behavior that would have gone on in the Globe. As the frustration level rises, stop the performers and the audience. Ask the audience to now behave in the conventional manner and have the performers try again. At an appropriate stopping point, ask which audience was easier to perform for. Why? Talk about what being a good audience means. Talk about audience behavior.

7. Read Shakespeare's work aloud. Pages 39-40 will provide an outline of how to make the words of this illustrious author come alive for students.

8. Clothing of the Elizabethan Era often provides great interest for students. The activities on pages 41-42 will allow students an opportunity to see how differently the people dressed than we do today. As an extension of this activity, students can design a costume for a favorite Shakespearean character.

Extending the Book

1. After reading the book, use the inquiry chart method as described in Enjoying the Book for other topics mentioned in the *Bard of Avon*. These include Queen Elizabeth, the theater, and Henry the IV. Find out more about the Commedia dell'Arte. (See page 69.)

2. Have students be aware of Shakespearean references in everyday life. Encourage them to share when they hear a quote or see an advertisement that features something that Shakespeare wrote. Page 33 lists some of the more familiar quotations.

3. Arrange a field trip to see a Shakespearean play. Check with local theater groups, college or high school drama departments, or a professional theater to see if they will be performing any Shakespeare. Sometimes it is possible to attend a dress rehearsal of a performance.

Shakespeare Survey

Shakespeare began writing and acting in plays 400 years ago, and his plays are being produced every day of every year somewhere. Some acting companies, such as the Royal Shakespeare Company of London and the Oregon Shakespeare Festival of Ashland, run his plays annually for the pleasure of millions of people. More than 21,000 musical compositions have been inspired by Shakespeare's plays and poetry, with *Hamlet* alone accounting for 1,405.

Very few people in the English-speaking world have not heard of Shakespeare, but there may be many who have never seen a play by Shakespeare. In small groups, or alone, survey your friends, teachers, family members, and neighbors, asking them the following questions:

	Yes	No
Have you ever heard of Shakespeare?		
Can you name at least one of his plays?		
Have you ever seen one of his plays?		
Have you ever seen a film made of one of his plays?		
Do you know the story of one of his plays?		

Record the answers you get in the chart above, then come back together as a class and combine your tallies. Make a bar graph of the answers you get on a poster or large sheet of paper and place on the class bulletin board. Record the class results in the chart below.

	Yes	No
Have heard of Shakespeare		
Can name one of his plays		
Have seen one of his plays		
Have seen film of a play		
Know story of a play		
Totals		

Survey of Sayings by Shakespeare

Sayings by Shakespeare fill almost ninety pages in *Bartlett's Familiar Quotations*. How many people can you find who have heard the following sayings or expressions? Place your tally marks in the blanks provided and combine your answers with those of your classmate's surveys.

Sayings	Have Heard	Have Not Heard
1. *To be or not to be, that is the question.*		
2. *A horse! A horse! My kingdom for a horse!*		
3. *All the world's a stage.*		
4. *What's in a name?*		
5. *Parting is such sweet sorrow.*		
6. *Household words*		
7. *What the dickens*		
8. *The primrose path*		
9. *Eaten me out of house and home*		
10. *Dead as a doornail*		
11. *An eyesore*		
12. *Foregone conclusion*		
13. *Bag and baggage*		
14. *A lean and hungry look*		
15. *Too much of a good thing*		
16. *The naked truth*		
17. *The game is up!*		

Scrambled Shakespeare

Oh, no! The "long and short of it" is that someone mixed up Shakespeare's biography and it's all scrambled. Read the sentences below. Then number them in the correct order.

As an extension, strips can be cut out and glued onto individual large sheets of paper. Have students illustrate the strips and assemble them into a Big Book. Make a cover and share the book as a review of Shakespeare's life.

	By 1594, Shakespeare had written five more plays and would write several more that year.
	After the births of his three children, Shakespeare moved to London, leaving his family behind.
	Shakespeare watched his first play when a group of traveling actors called the "Queen's Players" came to town in 1569.
	The plague broke out in London and all the theaters were closed for two years. Shakespeare wrote two long poems that he dedicated to the Earl of Southampton.
	When he was 18 years old, he married Anne Hathaway, who was 26 years old. They had three children.
	After James I became King of England, Shakespeare wrote *Macbeth*, a story from Scottish history because James was also King of Scotland.
	Shakespeare graduated from Stratford's Grammar School when he was sixteen. There was no money for the University, so he went to work.
	In 1599, the building of a new theater, named the Globe was a great event in Shakespeare's life and would be a name forever linked with his.
	When Shakespeare was 47, he retired to Stratford. He wrote his last few plays from there. They are gentle and full of love for the countryside.
	Southampton paid Shakespeare a lot of money for his poems. He invested the money in James Burbage's acting company, the Lord Chamberlain's Men.
	After the Globe Theater burned and was eventually rebuilt, William Shakespeare did not write any more plays. He died on April 23, 1616.
	In 1592, Shakespeare wrote a play, Henry VI, and acted in it. It was good enough to make the famous playwrights very jealous.

To Be or Not to Be....

Write a resumé for William Shakespeare to present to James I, the new King of England after Queen Elizabeth's death. Give vital statistics that will help the King learn about this phenomenal man. Use information in the book to complete the following form.

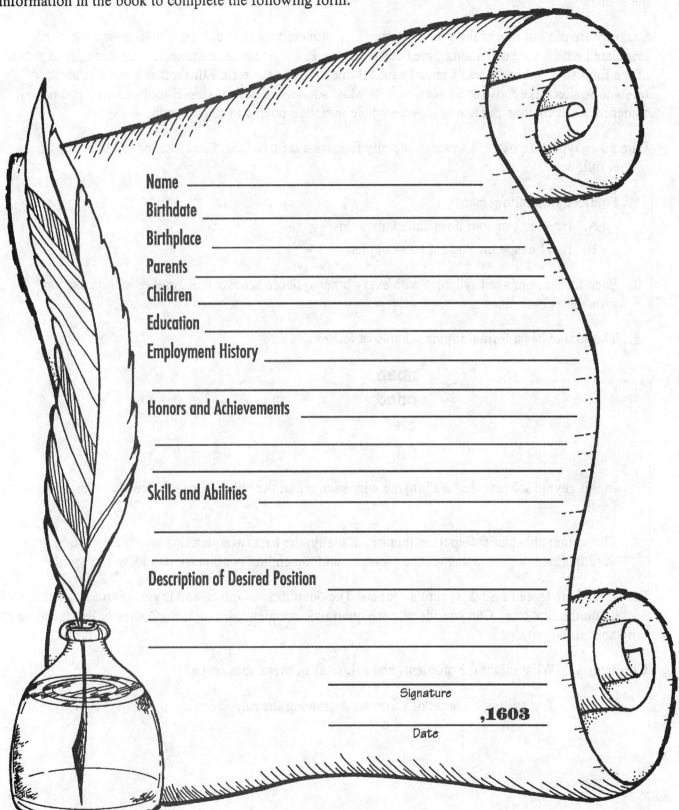

Name _____

Birthdate _____

Birthplace _____

Parents _____

Children _____

Education _____

Employment History _____

_____

Honors and Achievements _____

_____

_____

Skills and Abilities _____

_____

Description of Desired Position _____

_____

_____

Signature

_____ ,1603

Date

Elizabethan Sonnets

During the Elizabethan Age an educated person was expected to write poetry and to be able to recite from memory the classical poems of Greece and Rome. A favorite type of poem written in English was the sonnet.

Shakespeare did not invent the sonnet; Petrarch, a 14th century poet did, but Shakespeare has been associated with it for such a long time because of the 154 sonnets he wrote which are considered some of the English-speaking world's most beautiful lines. When the term Elizabethan sonnet is used, it refers to sonnets like those of Shakespeare's. Most sonnets consist of single, fourteen-line poems, but sometimes Elizabethan poets would write whole narrative poems in sonnet form.

Like many types of poetry, a sonnet generally follows a set of rules. The rules for the structure of a sonnet follow.

1. Fourteen lines altogether
   A. three sets of four lines called quatrains.
   B. two lines at the end called a couplet.

2. Each line contains ten syllables with every other syllable accented, beginning with the second syllable on each line.

3. The sonnet has a formal rhyme scheme as follows.

   abab

   cdcd

   efef

   gg

   In this rhyme scheme the "a's" rhyme with each other, the "b's" rhyme with each other, and so forth.

4. The sonnet also has a thematic structure. Usually, the first two quatrains set up a problem, the third quatrain begins to answer the problem, and the ending couplet tries to solve the problem.

On page 37 are three of Shakespeare's sonnets. The quatrains, couplets, and rhyme plan are identified for you on the first one. Can you identify the quatrains, couplets, and rhyme schemes of the second and third sonnets?

Challenges: What might the problems and solutions of these sonnets be?

Try writing a sonnet of your own following the rules above.

Shakespearean Sonnets

116

Let me not to the marriage of true minds   a
Admit impediments. Love is not love   b
Which alters when it alteration finds,   a
Or bends with the remover to remove.   b
Oh no! It is an ever-fixed mark   c
That looks on tempests and is never shaken.   d
It is the star to every wandering bark,   c
Whose worth's unknown, although his height be taken.   d
Love's not Time's fool, though rosy lips and cheeks   e
Within his bending sickle's compass come.   f
Love alters not with his brief hours and weeks,   e
But bears it out even to the edge of doom.   f
If this be error and upon me proved,   g
I never writ, nor no man ever loved.   g

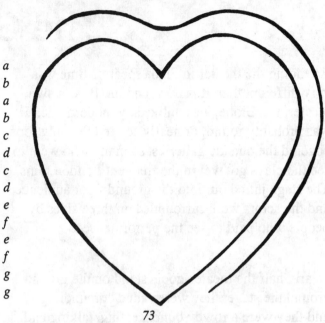

73

That time of year thou mayst in me behold
When yellow leaves, or none, or few, do hang
Upon those boughs which shake against the cold,
Bare ruined choirs* where late the sweet birds sang.
In me thou see'st the twilight of such day
As after sunset fadeth in the west,
Which by and by black night doth take away,
Death's second self, that seals up all in rest.
In me thou see'st the glowing of such fire,
That on the ashes of his youth doth lie
As the deathbed whereon it must expire,
Consumed with that which it was nourished by.
This thou perceiv'st, which makes thy love more strong,
To love that well which thou must leave ere long.

106

When in the chronicle of wasted time
I see descriptions of the fairest wights*,
And beauty making beautiful old rhyme
In praise of ladies dead and lovely knights,
Then, in the blazon* of sweet beauty's best,
Of hand, of foot, of lip, of eye, of brow,
I see their antique pen would have expressed
Even such a beauty as you master now.
So all their praises are but prophesies
Of this our time, all you prefiguring,
And, for* they looked but with divining* eyes,
They had not skill enough your worth to sing.
For we, which now behold these present days,
Have eyes to wonder, but lack tongues to praise.

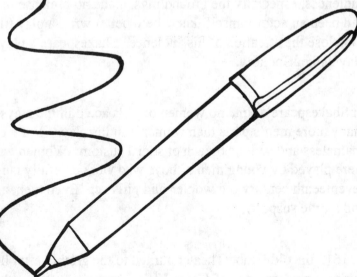

*choirs: part of a church; wights: men; blazon: praise; for: except that; divining: foreseeing

Attending Shakespeare's Theater, The Globe

Attending the theater in Shakespeare's time was very different than it is now, and the Bard's own theater, the Globe, was unlike any modern one. It was probably round, or nearly so, and the only roof covered the outside galleries, so many who went to see the plays got wet in the frequent London rains. The stage jutted out into the ground floor audience, and the actors were surrounded on three sides by people who paid to see the performance.

Nearly half the theater-goers stood on the ground around the stage; they were called "groundlings," and they were a rowdy bunch, eating, talking and yelling out anything which took their fancy at the moment. People paying higher prices got seats in the galleries for their money and a roof to keep off the rain.

No one went to the theater at night. There were no electric stage lights, and the stage was right out in open sunlight in the middle of the audience. There was no scenery and very few props. There were no costumes except for any which the actors had acquired for themselves, so there might be all manner of styles and periods of dress on the stage at one time.

Today no courteous theater-goer would think of walking around while a play was on, but Shakespeare's audiences, especially the groundlings, made no pretense of courtesy, and the playwriter, who after all had been an actor himself, knew he'd better write a play filled with action and good stories, or he would soon lose the attention of his audience. Shakespeare's plays are action-packed with all sorts of sword play and buffoonery.

In Shakespeare's time no women or girls acted in the plays, which is probably the main reason there are many more men's parts than women's in his plays. For women to act in a play would have been a shameless and serious breach of social custom. Women were played by men; girls and young women were played by young men or boys who were carefully taught by the older actors. Not until the late seventeenth century did women and girls act. Even then, an actress was considered somewhat daring and a little suspect.

In 1613 the old Globe Theater burned to the ground after being set on fire by a spark from a cannon during a performance of *Henry VIII*. Throughout the world today there are many Shakespearean festivals held in theaters that resemble the Old Globe theater.

Reading Shakespeare Aloud

The actor, Richard Burton, once said he loved the sound of Shakespeare's words because they made "such a beautiful noise." When he said this, he was referring to the way in which Shakespeare's words come alive musically when they are spoken aloud.

All of Shakespeare's plays and all of his poetry were written to be said aloud, and it is sometimes difficult for a newcomer to his works to get a true sense of how truly rich and lovely they are without learning first how his words sound. The Elizabethans loved the spoken word. When they went to a play, they went to listen, much as you would listen to a play on the radio, and not so much to see it. This is one reason Shakespeare's plays are full of puns, which are plays on words, and double entendres, which are words with two meanings with one meaning often improper or indelicate.

Learning to read Shakespeare aloud is not as difficult as it might seem with all its unfamiliar words. The reason they are unfamiliar to us is that they are no longer used much or at all. Some hints on how to read *Romeo and Juliet* aloud might help.

1. If possible, watch a film version of the Shakespearean play. Listen to what is said and how it is said. This will help you get a feel for the rhythm of the play. Rhythm is very important when reading Shakespeare. Some words should be said quickly; others, slowly. Try to understand the meaning of what is being said and let yourself get into the flow of the rhythm. You will probably understand more than you first thought you would.

2. You will certainly want to learn the meaning of some of the words with which you are unfamiliar. With many you can figure out the general intent without having to spend so much time in the dictionary you forget what has happened in the story. When you can't figure it out, look in the footnotes or glossary for help.

3. When in doubt about how to say a line, remember that the greatest stress of a line usually comes at the end of the sentence. An example of this is a line in Romeo and Juliet which may be misunderstood if it is spoken incorrectly. "Wherefore art thou Romeo?" is sometimes said with an accent on the word "art," when the accent should be placed on the name, "Romeo." Accenting the first word of this sentence suggests that Juliet is asking where Romeo is, when, in fact, she is asking, "Why are you named Romeo? Why are you the son of my family's enemy?"

(continued on page 40)

Reading Shakespeare Aloud *(cont.)*

4. Pay close attention to punctuation. When a line ends with a period, stop. If it ends with a comma, pause but do not completely stop. If the line does not end with punctuation, continue reading without stopping or pausing. You'll be amazed at how much better you understand what is said.

5. When an "ed" at the end of a word has an accent mark over it, pronounce the "ed" as a separate syllable. This will not change the meaning of the word, but it will continue the rhythm of the passage.

One last word on the meaning of Shakespeare's words. The words which you have the most trouble with will probably be the ones which we use today but give different meanings to than they had in Elizabethan times. Some examples of these in *Romeo and Juliet* are the following:

> *marry* was an oath meaning "by the Virgin Mary"
>
> *soft* meant "hold," "enough," or "wait a minute"
>
> *heavy* meant "sorrowful"
>
> *envious* meant "malicious"
>
> *sadly* meant "seriously"
>
> *happy* meant "fortunate"
>
> *still* meant "always"
>
> *anon* meant "soon"

Activity Suggestions

Choose one of the following activities to do in appropriately sized groups.

1. Do a Reader's Theater activity. In groups of three or four, choose a passage from *Romeo and Juliet* or one of Shakespeare's sonnets to read aloud. Decide which person will do which part, practice reading the selection until you know it well, and perform it for the class.

2. In groups of three or four, one person takes the part of the "reader" and reads a selection while the others act it out.

3. Choose a passage and translate it into "modern English"; then act it out.

Clothing of the Time

Men's Clothing

In Elizabeth's time men's clothing was as colorful as the ladies', but men wanted to look manly, so they wore clothing in the shape of armor, with broad shoulders, broad hips, and narrow waists. It could be compared with a suit of armor. After reading the descriptions, label the parts of the clothing.

- **Doublet:** like breastplate, covers back and chest, ridge down front; "wings" at shoulders
- **Sleeves:** separate garments, tight at wrists
- **Hose:** covered body from waist down
- **Ruff:** stiffly starched ruffles at neck, usually white
- **Hats:** of many different shapes, usually had bands around them, worn indoors
- **Cloaks:** capes
- **Gowns:** like a cloak, but closed in front, fitted at shoulders

The doublet was stuffed with horsehair, wool, or rags so it would keep its shape. The sleeves were tied to the doublet with laces The upper part of the hose was stuffed to make them stick out. Sometimes breeches, or "Venetians," were worn over the hose. Cloaks, worn over the doublet, were very fashionable and made in different lengths but usually short. Hats were worn indoors to keep warm.

Clothing of the Time *(cont.)*

Women's Clothing

Elizabethan women wanted their clothing to look much like the men's with broad shoulders, wide hips, and slim waists. Compare the drawing below to that of men's clothing and notice how similar it was to that of Elizabethan men's except for the kirtle. Women's dresses were not made all in one piece as they usually are today. Instead, women wore two or more garments as one "dress." After reading the descriptions, label the parts of the clothing.

- **Bodice:** came down to the waist; to make shoulders appear wide the bodice had "wings" and came to a point at the narrow waist

- **Sleeves:** separate garments held to bodice with laces; tight at wrists, but full otherwise. Stuffed to keep shape; sometimes had ruffs at wrists to match ruff at neck

- **Kirtle:** skirt often of different material from bodice; framework underneath called farthingale, made of wire or whalebone, caused kirtle to stand out from the body

- **Headwear:** Hats and hoods very popular; sometimes came to a point over the middle of the forehead, giving face a heart shape; styled very much like men's hats

- **Hair:** Worn in many different styles but always brushed back from forehead

- **Outer garments:** Cloaks and gowns like the men's; often wore a "safeguard," or overskirt, as well, to protect the kirtle, especially when riding horseback.

Great Renaissance Artists

Michelangelo Buonarroti was one of the great artists of the Renaissance. His fame began almost 500 years ago in Florence, Italy. He, along with Donatello, Leonardo, and Raphael are all well-known artists from the Renaissance era.

Renaissance means "rebirth." It was during the years 1400 to 1650 that Europe experienced a "rebirth" of interest in literature, trade routes, inventions, and new ideas about art. Cities began to expand and prosper. Explorations around the world brought back ideas and riches. Kings and queens ruled great empires. Art and architecture flourished.

Michelangelo, Donatello, Leonardo, and Raphael all lived during this time period. Donatello was one of the greatest sculptors of his time. He carved statues in marble but also cast them in bronze. Raphael was a very gifted painter and architect. He also did many frescoes, or wall paintings. Leonardo da Vinci was a writer, inventor, engineer, scientist and painter. His most famous painting is the Mona Lisa. Michelangelo was one of the greatest sculptors and painters in Europe. He was also an architect of churches, palaces, and fortresses. Michelangelo and Leonardo worked together on a project creating large battle scenes for walls of the city hall in Florence. From Leonardo, Michelangelo learned to show flowing and vibrant movement. Together, with many other Renaissance artists, these four created some of the most famous art in the world.

What did Michelangelo, Donatello, Leonardo, and Raphael all have in common? _____

_____

Using a dictionary, or other resource, match the terms to their descriptions.

_____ 1. Michelangelo   C. A time in history with a "rebirth" of new ideas.

_____ 2. Sculptor   I. To use a mold to form a statue.

_____ 3. Architect   P. A person who designs buildings.

_____ 4. Inventor   S. An architect of many churches.

_____ 5. Italy   B. A painting done on a wet wall.

_____ 6. Fresco   E. A person who imagines new ideas.

_____ 7. Statue   R. The country where all four artists lived.

_____ 8. Cast in Bronze   T. An artist who carves statues.

_____ 9. Scholar   L. An educated person.

_____ 10. Renaissance   A. A carved object.

Many churches and cathedrals were built during the Renaissance. Use your matching answers to discover the name of the church Donatello and Michelangelo designed together.

___ ___ , ___ ___ ___ ___ ___ ___ ___ ___ ___ ___ ___ ___ ___
1 2   3 4 2 4 5 1   6 7 1 8 9 8 10 7

Michelangelo

Michelangelo devoted his whole life to the creation of magnificent works of art. He was born in Caprese, Italy, on March 6, 1475, as Michelangelo Buonarroti. On that day, his father saw lucky stars in the sky and believed his son would have heavenly powers. For that reason, he named his son Michelangelo—angelo in Italian means angel.

Michelangelo was sent to school to become a scholar, but he was interested only in sketching and painting. He wanted to become an artist. His father and uncles were outraged. They thought art was an occupation only for peasants. They cruelly tried to change Michelangelo's mind, but that only made him more determined to succeed at art. Finally, when Michelangelo was 13, his father agreed to let him study with Domenico Ghirlandaio, a popular Florence painter.

In Florence, Michelangelo studied the art of the old masters and learned to paint frescoes, paintings done on wet plaster walls. Michelangelo was highly skilled and soon began to scorn others less skilled than he. He became hot-tempered and outspoken.

When Michelangelo was 16, he was sent to study sculpture under the talent of Bertoldo de Giovanni. Within two years, he had met the most outstanding men of the day and learned a great deal. He began to love the size and power of the Greek style of sculpture and became obsessed with trying to create perfect human forms in marble. He studied anatomy, the structure of the human body, and even secretly cut up dead bodies to see how they were put together. Sculpture became his mission in life.

Two years later, Michelangelo traveled to Rome. Here he created his first famous piece of art, the Pietà, a statue of Jesus and Mary. By 1501, he had become famous. He was 26 years old! His next statue was the warrior, David. He was then commissioned to do other work, designing tombs and libraries and painting frescoes.

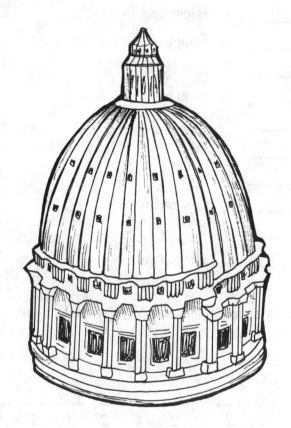

When Michelangelo was 30, he was asked by Pope Julius II to design his tomb. It was so large, a church had to be constructed around it! The church was St. Peter's Basilica. It took Michelangelo 40 years to construct the tomb and supervise work on the church. In the meantime, Michelangelo was asked to paint the ceiling of the Sistine Chapel within St. Peter's Basilica. Using a scaffold and lying on his back, Michelangelo took four years to finish painting this ceiling.

It is said that when Michelangelo was 60, he could still carve faster than three ordinary sculptors. Michelangelo lived to be 89, working steadily until his death in Rome on February 18, 1564. All his life he lived for his art and fulfilled the prophecy of the stars.

The Sistine Chapel

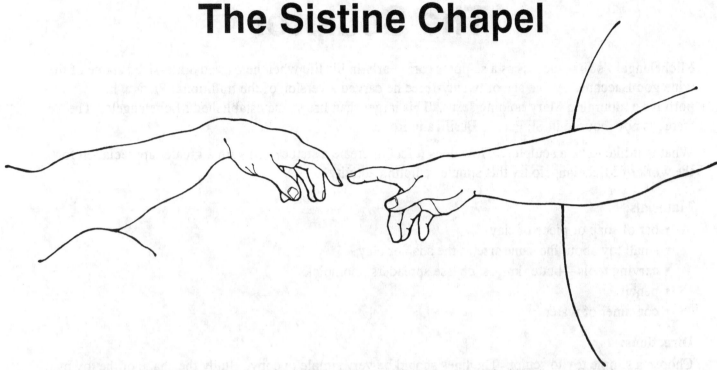

In 1508, Michelangelo began his most famous painting. He was commissioned to paint a fresco, a painting done on wet plaster, on the 10,000 square foot ceiling of the Sistine Chapel inside St. Peter's Basilica. In the picture, you can see the specially designed scaffold, which enabled Michelangelo to lie on his back to reach the ceiling. He worked long and hard on this project, locking out his assistants and doing all the work himself. He lay for hours at a time, with paint dripping into his eyes. He even slept in his clothes to save time. Despite the pleas from the Pope to finish quickly, and with almost non-stop painting, Michelangelo spent four years painting this magnificent work of religious art. The Sistine Chapel is still viewed today by over 7,000 people per day. It has recently undergone restoration and cleaning. The cleaning of *The Last Judgement,* which is on the wall above the altar, took four years. That is as long as it took Michelangelo to paint the whole ceiling!

Can you create pictures like Michelangelo? Now is your chance!

Materials needed:
- 12" by 18" (30 cm x 46 cm) white drawing paper
- pencil
- coloring materials (crayons, pens, pencils, pastels, or paints, etc.)
- tape

Preparation:
Take the piece of drawing paper and tape it under your desk, table, or chair.

Create:
Lie on your back under the paper and draw a picture. Try a castle scene, the streets of London in the 1600's, or one of your own choice. Add plenty of details and color. Do not forget your signature! And remember, you are lying down; do not expect perfection. When you finish, remove your picture and display in class (maybe on the ceiling).

Imagine! Michelangelo spent four years of his life on his back painting a ceiling. What kind of problems do you think he faced?

The Sculptor

Michelangelo's first success as a sculptor came early in his life when he carved a life-sized statue of the wine god Bacchus. At the age of twenty-three he carved a version of the traditional Pietà, which portrays a mourning Mary holding Jesus. This larger than life statue established Michelangelo. The statue is now housed in St. Peter's Basilica in Rome.

What is it like to be a sculptor? How does it feel to create a statue? To gain a greater appreciation for the work of Michelangelo try this simple sculpting activity.

Materials:

- bar of soap or piece of clay
- small toy about the same size as the soap or clay
- carving tools—butter knives, cheese spreaders, toothpicks
- pencil
- container of water

Directions:

Choose a simple toy to sculpt. The lines should be very simple to copy. Study the shape of the toy by both looking closely at it and holding it in your hand. Turn it over so you can see how it is made. Place it nearby where it is clearly visible.

Take the soap or clay and study it. Determine where you will begin your sculpting. Use the tip of a carving tool or a pencil and outline the areas you wish to carve away.

Cut into the soap or clay. Take your time, taking out small pieces first. If you need to soften the soap to make it easier to manipulate use a small amount of water on it.

When you have finished the outline, use whatever carving tools you can to create a smooth finish for your project.

Display it next to the toy you attempted to copy.

Leonardo da Vinci

Leonardo da Vinci was also a Renaissance painter, like Michelangelo. His famous works of art include *The Last Supper* and *The Mona Lisa*. Historians think he was born outside the village of Vinci, near Florence, Italy, in 1452. Leonardo was interested in and well-informed about many subjects—painting, sculpture, math, the human body, plant and animal life, and architecture. He was unable to go to school, so he taught himself. He sketched everything he saw and imagined. Today over 4,000 of his sketches and notes still exist. So other people would not be able to read his ideas, Leonardo wrote in "mirror writing".

Can you decipher this message?

More than 4,000 pages of
his notes and drawings
are still around. To read
them, people must hold them
up to a mirror. As a code,
he wrote all of the words
backwards!

Can you write your full name in "mirror writing"? Try it here.

Leonardo kept notebooks. In these he recorded his scientific observations. Try keeping a notebook for two weeks. Use it to write down any thoughts, observations, or ideas you may have. Sketch pictures of what you see. At the end of two weeks review your notebook. Think about what you have seen and what you have written.

The people of the Renaissance set very high goals for themselves. Leonardo da Vinci was one person who came close to reaching his goals. In your notebook, write some goals that you would like to achieve. Then set about doing what must be done to accomplish them.

The human body math activity on pages 56-57 and the aircraft science activities on pages 60-61 will also help you learn more about areas that da Vinci was interested in.

Renaissance Poetry

There were many famous poets from the Renaissance era. Some of them are listed below. Find some samples of their work in the library or resource books. Read some of the poetry aloud. Then follow the directions below for making aged paper. Copy one of their poems, a Shakespearean sonnet, or a poem of your own, onto the aged paper.

Garcilaso de la Vega, (c. 1501-1536)

Juan Boscán, (c. 1492-1542)

Luiz de Camões, (1524-1580)

Philip Sidney, (1554-1586)

Christopher Marlowe, (1564-1593)

John Donne, (1572-1631)

Robert Herrick, (1591-1674)

Thomas Wyatt, (1503-1542)

Edmund Spenser, (1552-1599)

Michael Drayton, (1563-1631)

Ben Jonson, (1572-1637)

George Herbert, (1593-1633)

Ludovico Ariosto (1474-1533)

Michelangelo Buonarroti (1475-1564)

Joachim du Bellay (1522-1560)

Pierre de Ronsard (1524-1585)

Making Aged Paper

Materials:

white, tan, or gray construction paper; tea bag; candle; cup; hot water; sponge; pens or markers; calligraphy pen (optional)

Directions:

1. Make a strong tea solution using one tea bag in ½ cup (125 mL) of hot water.

2. Dip a corner of the sponge in the strong tea and wipe over the paper to stain it.

3. Tear the edges of the paper in several places. Make the tears ½ to 1 inch (1.25-2.5 cm) deep.

4. **Note:** This step requires teacher supervision. Over a sink carefully use a lighted candle to singe the edges of the paper. If the paper begins to flame, use the sponge to smother it or drop it in the sink.

5. Allow the paper to dry.

6. Carefully write your poetry sample on the dried paper, using pens, markers, or a calligraphy pen.

Map of Renaissance Europe

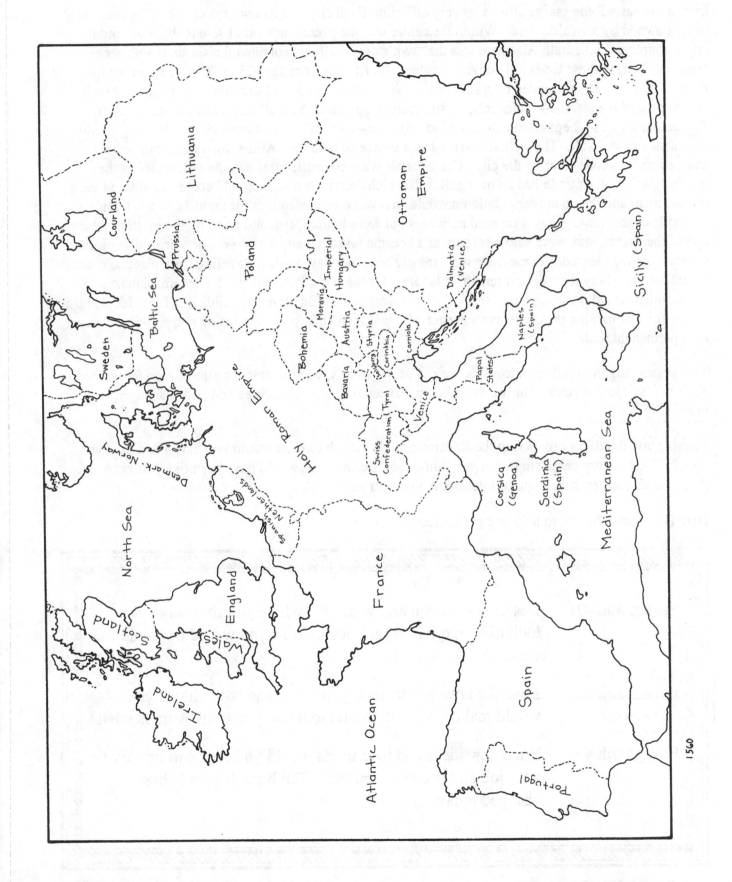

Hear Ye! Hear Ye!

Life in the early Renaissance cities was very difficult. Each city had its own system of self-government or was owned by a wealthy lord. Within the center was the piazza, or central square, built around the city's church or cathedral. Also here was the town's great bell that sounded the alarm of approaching enemies. During these times, all activities halted. All fit men from ages 15 to 70 were expected to fight. The city was surrounded by a large wall. New walls were added as cities expanded. The walls also separated the classes—merchants, master craftspeople, and the well-to-do lived on the insides. The poorer classes—beggars, outcasts, and journeymen—would live in houses or hovels built around the outside of the wall. The wall also served as a source of revenue. At the town gate, tolls were charged on all goods entering the city. Craftspeople were controlled through the strict rules of the guilds. Each craft or trade had its own guildhall which determined who could become an apprentice, a journeyman, and then a master. Children would first work as apprentices for up to 12 years, learning the skills of the trade. They were paid no wages but were housed, fed, and ruled by the master. At the end of their term, they were paid a set sum and became journeymen. They were now free to work for whomever they pleased. Journeymen were mostly hired out day-by-day, traveling from place to place to find work. Many journeymen remained laborers for the rest of their lives. To become a master, a journeyman would present a "masterpiece" of his work to be judged by the guildhall. They decided if it was worthy of naming the craftsman a master who was then able to acquire his own apprentices and set up a permanent trade.

This system began to fall apart towards the end of the 1600's, when guildhalls allowed too few masters and too many journeymen. During the following Industrial Age, both cities and trades changed drastically.

Imagine you lived in a city during the Renaissance. What job or craft would you have liked to have done? Write a story describing what you think your life and craft would have been like 400 years ago. Add a small picture, shop sign, or interesting border to your work.

Here is a sample format to help you get started:

Paragraph #1: Describe who you are, your age, where you live, what you look like. Explain what trade or craft you would have and why.

Paragraph #2: Describe how you learned your craft and what things you would make. What steps and tools do you think were needed?

Paragraph #3: What new ideas and inventions would you create to improve your job and become a master? Tell how that trade has changed today.

Picture This!

During the Renaissance, people worked hard for what they needed or wanted. The most highly-skilled workers made things by hand. Cut out the cards on pages 51-52. Match the job, the definition, and the picture cards to each other.

Job Name Cards

blacksmith	cutler	herbalist
minter	peddler	pewterer
porter	potter	poulterer
puppeteer	spinner	town crier
	weaver	

Job Definition Cards

1. walked through the town calling out the latest news	2. worked at his forge making horseshoes, weapons, and tools	3. sold and repaired knives, swords, and other cutting instruments
4. traveled from town to town selling everything	5. made coins from different metals	6. carried packages since the streets were too narrow for carts
7. shaped clay on a spinning wheel into jars and pots	8. worked with different kinds of puppets made from wood and cloth	9. made wool into thread

Picture This! *(cont.)*

10. gathered and sold plants to be used in medicines and cooking	11. raised chickens and other poultry to sell in the marketplace	12. wove thread into fabric to be used for clothing

13. melted pewter into shapes for keys, candlesticks, and pitchers	

Job Picture Cards

52

Signs of the Times

Most people during the Renaissance could not read or write. Shop merchants would use pictures carved on wooden signs to show their crafts or service. Label these signs below with the service you think they might provide. On the blank sign, draw a symbol and label it for another service of your choice.

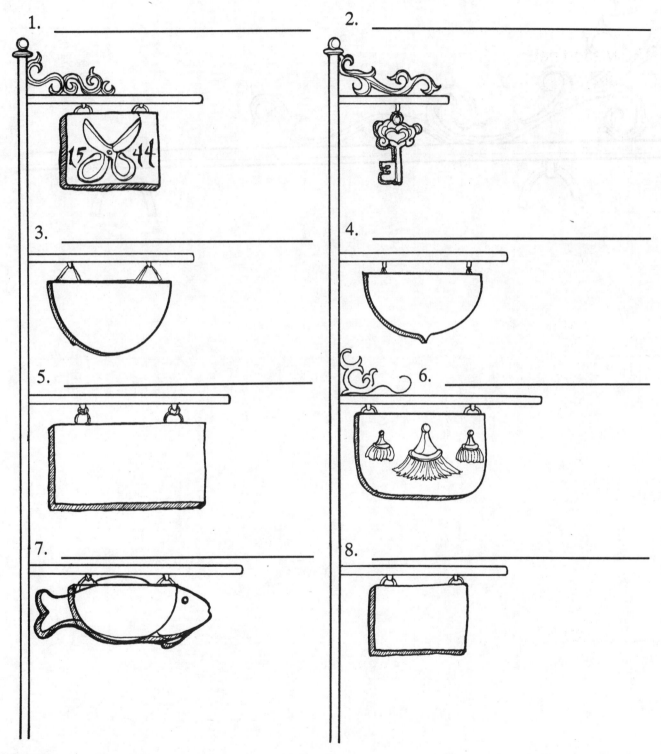

1. _____

2. _____

3. _____

4. _____

5. _____

6. _____

7. _____

8. _____

Hint:
The signs include a tailor, locksmith, brushmaker, and fishmonger.

Signs of the Times *(cont.)*

On this page, design a shop sign for a modern-day craft or service. Add detail and color, but no words.

Time Lines

Clothesline Time Line

Materials

- clothesline, string, or fishing line
- large index cards or rectangular white paper
- paper clips or clothespins

Directions

1. Hang the line across a section of the room. Make sure students can reach and see it easily.

2. Choose a main topic for the classroom and then make each student responsible for one item under the topic heading. There are many ways they can choose their items:
   A. List the choices on the board and have students sign up for one they like.
   B. Assign a specific topic to each student.
   C. Put all the choices in a container and have students draw their topics.

3. Allow research time.

4. Give each student a piece of rectangular paper. Fold it in half. On one side they draw a picture of their person, event, or item. On the other side, they write the date involved and a short summary about their topic.

5. Place their papers over the string. Hold them in place with a paper clip or clothespin.

Individual Time Lines

1. Assign or have students choose main topics to plot on a time line. They can use words, or a combination of pictures and words, to show the different items under their topics. Allow them access to some research materials and time to take notes.

2. Give each student a large piece of plain paper. Have them draw a time line across the center. Let them use their measuring and math skills to divide the line into the sections needed for their time period. Have them add their words and pictures above and below the time line in an eye-pleasing arrangement. They may wish to draw the pictures and type the words on separate pieces of paper to be cut and glued onto the large paper.

Time Line Topic Ideas

1. Events from each of the books used in this unit
2. The life of William Shakespeare
4. Artists from the Renaissance
5. Explorers
6. The life of Leonardo da Vinci
7. Inventions and their inventors
8. Famous people who lived during the years 1400 - 1600
9. Events that were happening in other parts of the world:

China and Japan   Aztecs, Mayas, and Incas
Africa
India

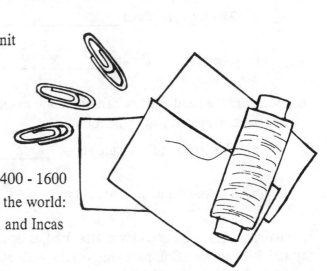

Human Body Proportions

Leonardo da Vinci and Michelangelo both studied the human body thoroughly in order to better reproduce human figures in their artwork. This famous sketch from da Vinci's notebook is often used as a symbol for the Renaissance.

Each student will need a copy of the skeleton on page 57 and a ruler to do the following activities.

1. Measure the length of the arm from the shoulder to the fingertips. _____

   Measure the length of the leg from the hip to the toes. _____

   What is the difference between the length of the arm and the leg? _____

2. Measure the width of the shoulders. _____

   Measure the width of the hipbones. _____

   What is the difference between the width of the hips and the shoulders? _____

3. Measure the length of the arm from the elbow to the fingertips. _____

   Measure the length of the arm from the shoulder to the elbow. _____

   Which part of the arm is longer? By how much? _____

4. Measure the length of the leg from the knee to the toe. _____

   Measure the length of the leg from the hipbone to the knee. _____

   Which part of the leg is longer? By how much? _____

5. Measure the length of the entire body from the top of the skull to the toes. Use previous measurements to complete the following:

   a. The legs are about _____ of the entire body height.
   (fraction)

   b. The arms are about _____ of the entire body height.
   (fraction)

6. Measure the head and neck from the top to where the neck meets the shoulders. Use previous measurements to answer the following:

   a. The head and neck are about _____ of the entire body height.
   (fraction)

   b. The head and neck are about _____ the length of a leg.
   (fraction)

Extensions: Trace around classmates' bodies on butcher paper. Use a yardstick or meter stick to do the activities above. Compare your results with each other. What generalizations can you make about human body proportions? Make a drawing of the human body using the correct proportions.

Human Body Proportions (cont.)

Use this skeleton to complete the activties on page 56.

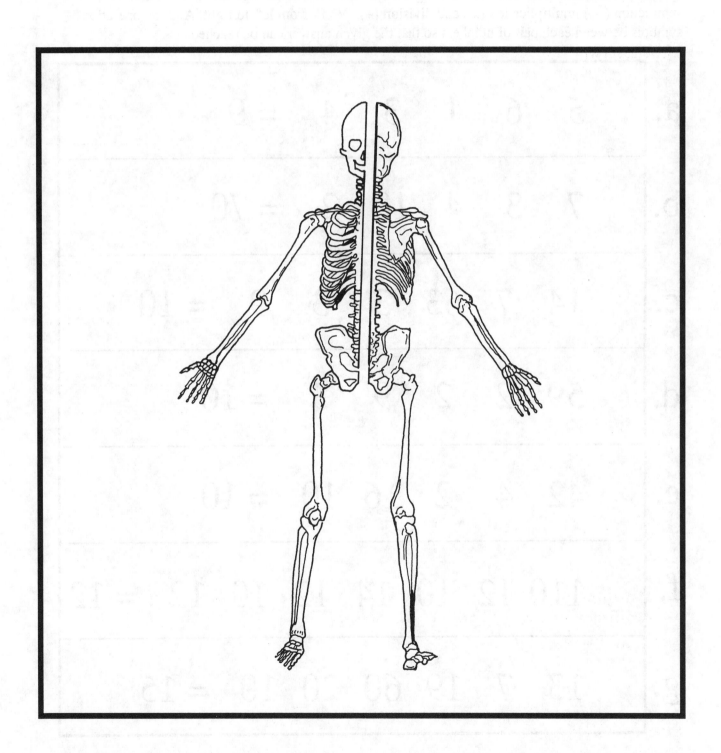

Math

The Importance of Math Symbols

During the Renaissance mathematical symbols were introduced. First used in 1537, the equal sign (=), the plus (+), and minus (–) sign helped the development of mathematics.

Try the problems below. They are missing the symbols for the four operations—addition (+), subtraction (—), multiplication (x), and division (÷). Work from left to right. Add the operation symbols between each pair of numbers so that the given answer can be reached.

a.	5 6 1 3 4 = 9
b.	7 3 4 10 2 = 70
c.	14 7 63 3 3 9 = 10
d.	59 2 2 9 3 = 10
e.	42 4 2 16 10 = 10
f.	110 12 10 14 12 10 12 = 12
g.	13 7 19 60 20 10 = 15

Challenge: Try writing some problems of your own leaving out the operation signs. Exchange them with classmates and solve.

Renaissance Science Experiences

The Renaissance is regarded as a time when science took on new significance. Try these experiences and talk about the outcomes.

Mystery Matter

Alchemists tried in vain to change ordinary metals into gold. However, it is possible to change some materials into something very different. To see this try the Mystery Matter experiment.

Materials

- borax (available where laundry detergents can be purchased)
- water
- white glue
- food coloring (optional)
- plastic spoons (1 per person)
- self-sealing sandwich bags (1 per person)
- paper towels for clean-up

Directions

Ahead of time, dissolve ½ cup (125 mL) of borax in 1 quart (.95 L) of very hot water. Set aside to cool.

Student Directions

Have students work in pairs so they can share spoons.

1. Put 2 spoonfuls of water into each self-sealing sandwich bag.
2. Add 3 spoonfuls of white glue. Share the same spoon so that you have a clean spoon to use later.
3. Seal the bag. Mix water and glue by squishing the bag.
4. Open bag and add 2 spoonfuls of borax solution. Use the clean spoon.
5. Seal the bag completely, pushing out excess air.
6. Observe changes carefully while squishing the mixture in the bag.
7. When thickened, remove Mystery Matter and roll in hand.

   Note: A polymer has been created.

Germs

During the Renaissance, people did not know that germs were the cause of disease. It was not until about 1590, when the microscope was invented that germs were also discovered. Let students see what germs are like by trying the activity below.

Use petri dishes with a growing medium already in them to have students grow bacteria from their own hands. Let them observe the bacteria through microscopes.

The dishes, with directions for conducting the activity, can be ordered from:

Carolina Biological Supply Company
2700 York Road
Burlington, NC 27215
1-800-334-5551

Leonardo da Vinci and Science

Leonardo da Vinci was the inventor and designer of some very unusual objects, though they could not be built with the materials of the times. Here are some of his sketches for inventions he envisioned.

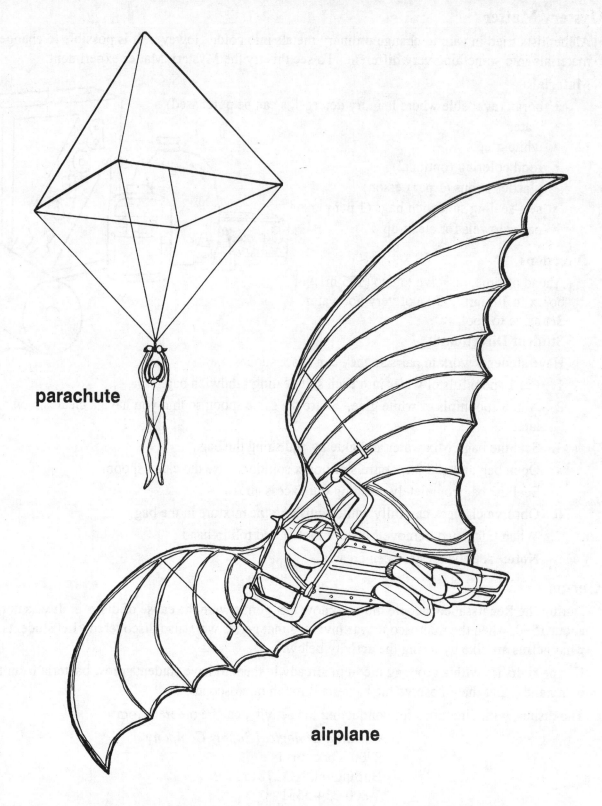

parachute

airplane

On page 61 there are some other unusual aircraft designs. Try some out and see how they work.

Paper Aircraft

Try making some of these paper aircraft by following the directions below.

The Rotor

Materials needed:

- construction paper in 6" (15cm) squares
- pencil
- ruler
- scissors

Directions:

- Using a pencil and ruler, make these patterns on your paper.
- Cut out and fly.

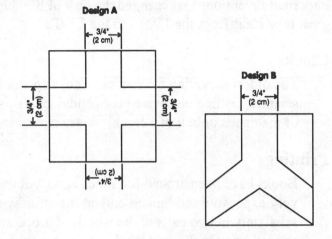

Twister

Materials needed:

- construction paper 3" by 7" (7.5cm x 18cm) or 5" by 8" (13cm x 20cm) index card

Directions:

- Using a pencil and ruler, make this pattern on your paper.
- Cut out, fold areas A and B down.
- Stand on your chair and drop the twister.

Does it always spin in the same direction?

Try to design one with 6 points. Does it fly?

The Loop

Materials needed:

- plastic, non-flexible straw
- paper strips
- tape

Directions:

- Using the picture as a model, create your own loop.
- Experiment with different size loops and the placement of the strips. Compare with other designs.

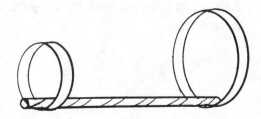

Inventions

The Renaissance was a time for wonderful new ideas and creative thought. This thinking led to some important inventions that changed the way of life during these years. Here is a list of only some of the great new ideas from the 1300's to the 1600's.

Clocks

The oldest surviving mechanical clocks appear to be from the late 1300's. In 1581, the Italian scientist Galileo discovered the pendulum. This enabled a better regulator for constant movement of the hands or bell of a clock. Water clocks and hourglasses were also widely used in the 1500's.

Printing

Books have been around for a long time, but they took months or years to hand print. They were very expensive and limited only to the wealthy and scholars. Block printing of books developed separately in two parts of the world—Europe and China. The Chinese produced the first block-printed book in 868 and the first movable type process in 1041. The Chinese made their type out of baked clay, but these could not withstand repeated use. The Koreans, in the early 1500's, developed a metal type that is still in use today. In the mid-1400's, in Europe, Johan Gutenberg invented the printing press, using movable type. Now books could be printed with greater speed and less effort. Information could be shared with more people. Once the materials became more available, more people became interested in studying, learning, and attending schools. His development was so efficient that there were no significant changes until automation was introduced in the 19th century.

Eyeglasses

Around the 1300's, paintings first appeared with the people wearing or holding spectacles. In the 1400's with the invention of the printing press and more books available, the demand for eyeglasses increased. It is thought that the first glasses for far-sightedness were developed in Italy in 1287. Later in the 1500's, near-sightedness was able to be corrected. The first glasses were crude, heavy, and made by hand. A variety of materials were used for frames including wood, lead, copper, bone, leather, and even horn in an attempt to make them lighter.

Lenses

After the development of eyeglasses, lenses were then used in other areas. In 1608, Hans Lippershey found that putting two lenses together magnified the image. Thus a working telescope was created, but the image was poor. Isaac Newton solved this problem in 1668, by making a reflecting telescope. In 1606, Galileo created the astronomical telescope to look at the stars and planets. He discovered the mountains on the moon and many new stars. Also in the mid-1600's, Anton van Leeuwenhoek by using many tiny lenses was able to magnify up to 200 times—the microscope.

62

Inventions *(cont.)*

Musket

The musket was the first usable rifle that soldiers could carry with them into battle. It was developed in Spain in the 1500's. It could fire a metal ball that could kill or seriously injure people. Before then, soldiers fought with swords, cannons, clubs, and hand weapons. The first muskets were very heavy, at 40 pounds (14k) and 6 feet (2 meters) long, and difficult to use. Soldiers, known as musketeers, often rested their guns on forked stands to improve accuracy. The suit of armor from the Middle Ages was no match for the musket, so the knight in shining armor disappeared.

Rudder

Around the 1200's, a number of inventions revolutionized water travel and made it possible for long voyages of exploration. One was the sternpost rudder. This greatly increased the control over the steering of the ship. Another was the tun, a wooden cask for water. Now with a fresh supply of water on board, a ship could take longer voyages from land. So important was the tun that a ship's carrying capacity was measured in "tunnage," meaning the amount of space on a ship. Today the word is spelled "tonnage", and still refers to the amount of space in shipping.

Wallpaper

Before the development of wallpaper, only the wealthy of medieval times could afford to adorn the walls of their castles with woven tapestries. The tapestries helped to keep the cold castle walls warmer, and told stories stitched in elaborate detail. The lower classes hung cheaper painted-cloth imitations on their interior walls. Then in 1496, England saw its first paper mill come into operation, and it soon became the site of innovative work by English artists. This lead to the production of wallpaper decorated with hand-painted designs, stencils, and wood-block prints. For the next 200 years, England was the premier producer of wallpaper for Europe.

The Flush Toilet

The water closet (one of many names for early flush toilets) dates back to 1589 when it was invented by Sir John Harington. The tank worked with a valve that released the flow of water. Harington recommended that it be flushed once or preferably twice a day.

Other Inventions	Inventor	Date	Place
Adding Machine	Blaise Pascal	1642	France
Air pump	Otto von Guericke	1654	Germany
Barometer	Evangelista Totticelli	1643	Italy
Thermometer	Galileo	1593	Italy
Watch (portable timepiece)	Peter Heinlein	1504	Germany

Is It New?

Read pages 62-63. Look at all the inventions that originated during the Renaissance. How many of them are still in existence today? Using one of the inventions listed, or others that you find out about, complete the following activity.

Then to Now Inventions

1. What is the invention?

    _____

2. Who is given credit for having invented it?

    _____

3. In what country did it originate?

    _____

4. In what year did it originate?

    _____

5. In a few well written sentences describe the invention as it was first known. Include any information that is important to its development.

    _____

    _____

6. How has this invention changed through the years?

    _____

    _____

7. Is it still used for the same purpose?

    _____

8. What are some present-day applications for this invention?

    _____

    _____

9. How do people today find out about this invention and its uses? Look through magazines and newspapers. Cut out articles or ads and staple them to this paper.

    _____

    _____

10. What do you see as the future of this invention?

    _____

    _____

Printing Simulations

To help students understand the role that technology plays in industry and to let them get a feeling for the importance of the invention of the printing press, conduct the following simulations.

Divide the class into groups of four to six. Each group should choose a simple design or object that they wish to reproduce. Following the directions below, blocks for printing the object singly and in sets should be made by each group.

Making Printing Blocks

Materials:
- pencil
- thick cardboard
- glue or rubber cement
- paper for printing on
- scissors
- squares and rectangles of wood
- tempera paints or inks
- a wide brush and large flat tray or cookie sheet (one for each color you use)

Directions:

1. On the thick cardboard, draw the simple shapes you want to print.

2. Cut out the shapes and glue them onto blocks of wood. Glue some alone onto a square block and some in rows onto rectangular blocks. Let them dry.

3. Put a few spoonfuls of paint onto the large trays. Spread the paint around with the wide brush so it covers the bottom of the tray with a thin layer.

4. To print, press the block of wood (with the shape side down) into the tray of paint. Press your painted block on the paper.

5. Repeat step 4 until you get the design you want.

(Continued on page 66.)

Printing Simulations *(cont.)*

Within each group, several methods of reproducing wrapping paper will be tried. Each student should have the opportunity to experience each method. Before beginning, the group should decide what their wrapping paper design will be. Records should be kept concerning the number of products produced, the quality of the product, and the amount of worker effort needed.

Method 1: Hand Reproduction

Students will hand draw and color the design onto the paper. This method parallels the hand copied and illustrated books prior to the invention of printing.

Method 2: Single Block Reproduction

Students will use a single block over and over again to reproduce the design onto the paper. This illustrates the beginning of the printing process. A page or design was carved onto a piece of wood, which could be used over and over again as long as that particular item was being printed. It would have to be discarded when its production was stopped.

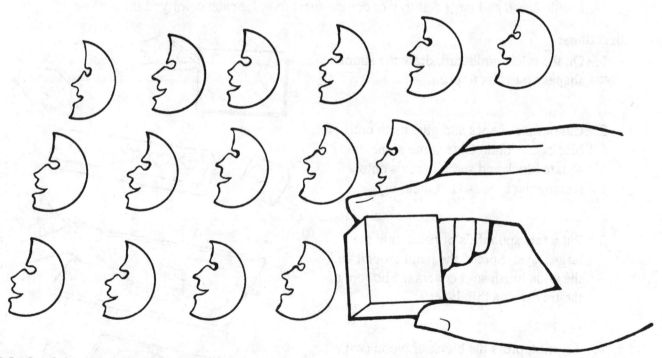

Method 3: Line Reproduction

Students will use the rectangular row of designs to reproduce the design onto the paper. This shows how combining single objects could make the printing process more efficient.

Method 4: Moveable Type

Students will combine and recombine single blocks created by several groups to show how a piece of "type" could be used over and over again to produce a variety of designs on paper. Select the desired blocks, arrange them in the desired pattern, tape them with duct tape into one block, and print the wrapping paper. Untape the blocks and reuse them to create new designs.

66

Great Minds Don't Think Alike...

The Renaissance was a time of great change and creativity. Here is a fun thinking activity you may want to try with your students. You will be surprised at the results!

Preparation: *You will need the following for each student:*

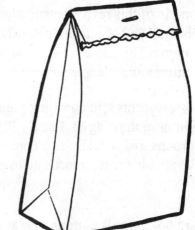

- paper lunch bag
- paper plate
- white paper napkin
- plain paper cup (any size)
- a piece of string—12 inches (30cm)
- a plastic spoon
- 4 toothpicks
- a copy of the rules below

- Place all the items inside the paper bag; close and staple.

- Hand each student a bag as they leave for the day, telling them to open it at home and follow the directions inside.

- Choose a date for the results to be brought back to class—2 to 3 days or a week later. Have a large table ready to display the finished products.

Great Minds Don't Think Alike

Test your creativity.

1. Inside this bag are 9 items that you can use in any way possible to create an object.

2. You can cut, bend, glue, or tape. You can even add color. CHALLENGE your mind to create something unusual or something you use everyday. What can it be?

3. You can use only the items in the bag. You may use all of them, some of them, or even parts. You can even ask your family for ideas.

4. Bring your projects back to school on _____.

Good luck!

A Renaissance Cathedral

Italian architects during the Renaissance looked back in time to ancient Rome for their inspiration and began to incorporate many Roman elements into their creations. St. Peter's Basilica in the Vatican City is a good example of this revivalist attitude and of Italian Renaissance architecture in general. Built between 1506 and 1660, St. Peter's Basilica had ten different architects including Michelangelo, who designed the dome. The dome is based on classical Roman architecture, as is the facade with its Corinthian columns and triangle structure.

For this project, students will construct their own Renaissance Cathedral, using their own Roman inspired design or replicating St. Peter's Basilica. This fun and creative project can be done in cooperative groups, individually as a home project, or as a class assignment. Have a supply of books and pictures available for reference and to provide ideas and styles.

Materials:

cardboard boxes (milk cartons, cereal boxes, shoe boxes etc.); tape; crayons or paints; markers; scissors; construction paper; graph paper; tissue paper; clear plastic wrap

Step 1: Planning

Most cathedrals were designed with a floor plan in the shape of a cross. With your group members, brainstorm and write down all the ideas your group can come up with: whether to replicate St Peter's Basilica, or what your own Renaissance cathedral would look like, materials to use, etc. Next, use graph paper to design your floor plan. Make up a supply list and decide who will bring which items from home. Check with your teacher first to see which items the school can supply.

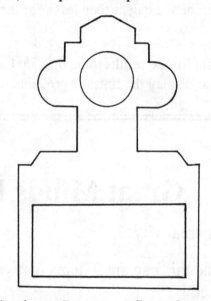

Step 2: Construction

You will need a large piece of cardboard as a building base. Draw your floor plan onto this base. Build the main structure first and then add domes, columns, towers, etc. A roof that comes off makes it easier to add details to the interior later.

Step 3: Details

Paint or cover with paper the exterior of your cathedral. Black or grey lines can be drawn to simulate stones. Add details to the interior, like stained glass windows, altars, etc.

Step 4: Presentation

Prepare a short speech for the class. Choose a spokesperson from your group. Tell the class which church you chose or if you designed your own, what are some of the features you adapted from ancient Roman buildings, and what were some of the construction problems.

Commedia dell'Arte

A new form of theater developed in Italy around 1550. This was the Commedia dell'Arte, and it quickly spread across Europe and England, lasting until the late 18th century. The Commedia dell'Arte actors were professional troupes who travelled from city to city performing for peasants and noblemen alike. They had a set of stock characters and an outline of a plot around which they improvised the dialogue and action. Each performer always played the same character, with its fixed attributes and costume. Harlequin, Pantaloon, and Pulcinella were some of the characters of the Commedia dell'Arte. Part of the costume of many of the characters was a half mask which covered the eyes, cheeks, and nose. The masks not only showed the personality of the character but drew more attention to the body movements of the actors.

Have students put on short improvised plays using masks and characters they create.

After writing a short character description, have students make half-masks with features that show the personality they described. Use the pattern on page 70 or they can design their own.

In small groups have the students outline a simple scenario for their play using the characters they created, making sure that each has a part. Have the students present their own Commedia dell'Arte performance.

Mask Pattern

Use this pattern to create half masks. These may be decorated and used in performing scenes from plays or worn at the Renaissance Faire. Use construction paper, scissors, scraps of material, ribbon, yarn, felt, foil, glitter, or paper to decorate. Determine where eye holes should be placed before beginning. Draw them and cut them out.

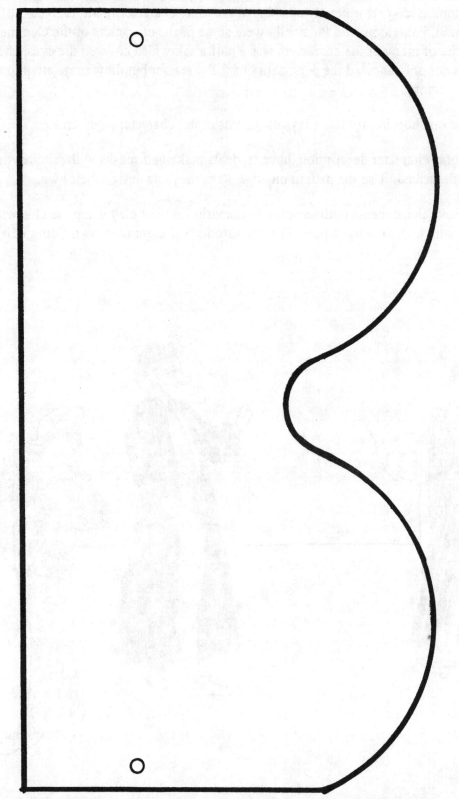

Renaissance Music

As with art, architecture, exploration, and literature, music also made some dramatic changes during the Renaissance era. The development of the violin, the flute, and the organ gave rise to a demand for new musical forms. Up until the 1600's, most music was written for and performed in churches. Now music was also written for theater and court entertainment. Below are some people, places, and things involved in these new changes.

The Court of Burgundy

Under the patronage of Phillip the Good and Charles the Bold during the 15th century, Guillaume Dufay and Gilles Binchois wrote many compositions. They wrote music for Masses in the Roman Catholic Churches, and popular songs called chansons. *Chansons* is French for songs. Written for several voices and two or more instruments, these were popular court entertainment.

Flemish Composers

Jean d'Ockeghem, Josquin des Prez, Heinrich Isaac, and Clement Janequin were all well-known for their excellent works in religious music, chorals, and chansons.

Madrigals

Around the 1500's, madrigals became popular. These were vocal settings of Italian poems. They were often about unrequited love and were intense and expressive. Luca Marenzio of Italy and Thomas Morley of England wrote many beautiful madrigals.

Ayres

This was another popular vocal form from England. The ayre was a song for a solo voice with a lute or viol accompaniment. Most of these were very serious and emotional.

Baroque Music

This term refers to music composed from 1600 to 1750. The music compositions were huge and elaborate, requiring great numbers of singers and players to perform them. It began in Florence, Italy, when a group wanted to revive the Greek drama. Instead, they produced something entirely new—opera. One of the most daring composers of this new time was Claudio Monteverdi.

Stringed Instruments

The lute was a popular stringed instrument at the beginning of the Renaissance. It is referred to in the beginning paragraph of *The High Voyage* and pictured on the "Women at Court" pages of *The Renaissance* by Tim Wood. By the late Middle Ages, simple bowed instruments began to appear, called viols. These were used to perform chamber music. By the early 16th century, the first violin appeared, and eventually the complete family: violin, viola, cello, and double bass. The development of the violin family enabled a greater range of music to be written. Antonio Stradivari (1644-1737) was the most famous of violin makers during the late Renaissance. His instruments, some of which are still in existence today, are prized collector items.

Organ Music

Renaissance composers like Giovanni Gabrieli and Jan Pieters Sweelinck wrote many pieces for the organ. Girolamo Frescobaldi perfected some of the main forms of organ music: the toccata, fugue, and partita.

Renaissance Music (cont.)

Find the words associated with Renaissance music in the puzzle below.

Ayres	Baroque	Burgundy	Chansons	Composers
Compositions	Instruments	Lute	Madrigals	Music
Opera	Organ	Renaissance	Stradivari	Viol
Chamber Music		Chorals	Violin	Vocal

```
B N S O L E L J Q Z D E T C G V S G R B Y H Q
C D C O I D A N L L E B O Q V O Q T E Q E G S
G A I V W G W A A W U M A A Y Q Q F U L O N Q
M V Y F K D C E L K P Q F T J L D I Z O B X I
S R L R T O R O N O D O O V I O L I N T A P L
T L F L V N B D S Q X Y O Z V H P B H Z D R S
R B A R E N A I S S A N C E D L Q X Z X T M W
A Y A G A P T O R S U U Z Y U X K K M Y I C Z
D X F Y I I F K L I U R Z Z J M B I S J O H R
I A Q P O R I M C H A N S O N S P H Y M Z A O
V H K N O K D B X E J P X G T F A B P Z Y M L
A H S T I S S A A T A R E P O E S O O M F B S
R X M M P Q E T M U B S T P N S S Z R S I E N
I J V C K K B X V L U E C E Y E Y E D L E R O
K D K O W T T C S R L R I P R M X R O A R M R
E O Y D N U G R U B X Y S S Z B Y D M R P U Z
A Q O V U Q B L V W M A U U Y F O L B O X S P
T Q F N G Z E U Z C Y J M Y O W R X M H P I S
Z Y Z U T X T U X Z X O J V H X G W Z C C C A
H O P Y X V Q O E U Q O R A B E A T V N D W S
I N S T R U M E N T S E G H M F N O L Z X X L
J E J K J N G H P M T T I C Q J E U I D L L B
```

72

Renaissance Foods

Since ancient times, salt has been very precious. It was used for both seasoning and preserving foods. During the Renaissance, salt was still used for preservation, but spices from new places were causing changes.

During the Middle Ages, Arabian traders brought new spices to Europe, and Europeans decided they wanted more. This set the scene for one of history's most famous voyages. Spice merchants could become very rich during the Renaissance. Cinnamon was worth its weight in gold. A sack of pepper was almost priceless. One pound of cloves could be exchanged for seven sheep or cows. Queen Isabella wanted to make her country rich, so she listened to the plans of a young man called Christopher Columbus.

Many of the new foods and plants that Columbus took to the New World had never been seen by the natives: foods like carrots, turnips and lettuce. The New World foods that Columbus took back to Spain were just as strange to the Europeans. Columbus did not find the black pepper he was searching for, but he did bring back allspice, a sharp spice made from a berry. He also brought back lima beans, maize (or corn), sugar cane, and cacao beans, from which chocolate is made.

During a Renaissance feast, you could find a variety of interesting foods. There was roast chicken, pork ribs, Cornish game hens, marinated quail, and steak on a stick. You could also find cheese and mushroom pies, Toad in a Hole (meats in a roll), Cornish pasties (meat and potatoes in pastry), bangers (large sausages), and piroshki (turnovers filled with meat and spices). For dessert, there was elderberry funnel cake, chocolate-dipped berries, and black pears with carob cream. To drink you could try ales, beers, and wines (watered down for children), Turkish coffees, spiced teas, and kefir.

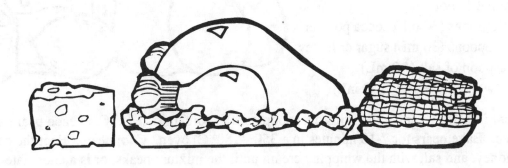

Renaissance Recipes

Here are two recipes to try. The ingredients have been modernized so they can be found easily.

Toad in a Hole

- 1 package refrigerated crescent rolls or croissant mix
- 1 pound (450 g) ground veal, pork, or chicken
- 1 cup (250 mL) bread crumbs
- 2 eggs
- pinch of mace, salt and pepper
- 1 tablespoon (15 mL) of parsley
- 1 tablespoon (15 mL) chopped shallots
- $\frac{1}{3}$ cup (83 mL) of whipping cream

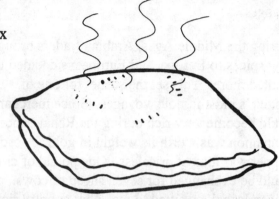

Preheat oven to 450º F/230º C. Mix dough as directed and spread into 4-6 rectangles. Mix remaining ingredients thoroughly and divide among rectangles. Roll dough around and over mixture. Seal edges. Brush with egg yolk to glaze. Bake for 20-25 minutes, or until golden brown. Serve with sweet, hot mustard. Makes 4-6 toads.

Pears with Chocolate Cream

- 6 fresh pears
- juice of 1 lemon
- 2 tablespoons (30 mL) cocoa powder
- 2 tablespoons (30 mL) sugar or honey
- ¼ teaspoon of salt (1.2 mL)
- 1 cup whipping cream (250 mL)

Cut the pear in half. Keeping the skins on, scoop out the core and seeds. Coat each pear half with lemon juice. Bake pears for 7-10 minutes in a 350º (180º C) oven. Cool pears. Beat the cocoa powder, sugar or honey, and salt with the whipping cream until the mixture peaks, or is a chocolate mousse consistency. Spoon mixture into the hollow core of each pear and chill for 30 minutes.

74

A Renaissance Faire

To culminate your Renaissance unit, you will want to plan a Renaissance Faire to celebrate and share your learning. Make this a time for showcasing your students work. It will allow you to assess at a glance what your students have synthesized in their learning.

The faire will take some advanced planning and organization. Allow students to do as much as possible from designing invitations and sending them to deciding which of their projects should be on display.

Begin by choosing a date, time, and place. Give yourself plenty of time to complete the unit as it will make the experience richer for the students. Since this should take place at the end of the unit, students can work on this as they study the Renaissance.

Decide where this will take place. Although your classroom is suitable, holding the faire outside would be appropriate. During the Renaissance the wealthy Italians particularly revived the love of the countryside.

Organize your class into committees and let them decide what would be best to highlight. Decide along with them whom to invite. Choose from the following activities.

Inventions

Students can choose an invention that was created during the Renaissance and explain it. They can then talk about how it has evolved and is used today. Ask the guests where they have seen or used the invention in their life.

Display the "Great Minds Don't Think Alike" creations. (page 67)

The Artists of the Time

Throughout the unit collect reproductions of artwork from the Renaissance. Intersperse them with work that the students have done. These include the banners on page 28 and the soap sculptures on page 46.

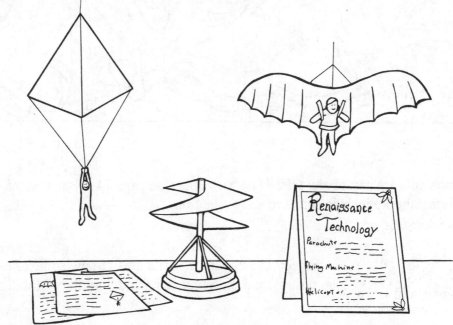

(continued on page 76)

A Renaissance Faire *(cont.)*

Drama

Present a scene or a reading from Shakespeare. Use the bibliography on pages 77-78 to find a selection. Create a replica of a mask that was used in the Commedia dell' Arte to wear while doing the presentation. You might show a clip from a video of a Shakespearean play.

Music

Play some music of the Renaissance. Some sources are listed in the bibliography on page 78. Stringed instruments became popular during the Renaissance. Invite students who play stringed instruments to play them or invite a string quartet to play for your faire.

Food

Refreshments are part of any faire. Use the recipes on page 74 or serve some of the foods on page 73. Remember to include spices to add to the fun.

Displays

Set up displays of student projects throughout the faire area. Show some of the time lines, cathedrals, the Guess Who posters, and the Sequencing and Summary Mobiles.

Bibliography

Fiction

Cervantes, Miguel de. retold and illustrated by Marcia Willings. *Don Quixote*.
  Candlewick Press, 1993.

Chaucer, Geoffrey. *Canterbury Tales*. Viking Child Bks., 1951.

Jacques, Brian. *Redwall*. Putnam Pub. Group, 1987.

Jacques, Brian. *Mossflower*. Putnam Pub. Group, 1988.

Jacques, Brian. *Mattimeo*. Putnam Pub. Group, 1990.

Jacques, Brian. *Mariel of Redwall*. Putnam Pub. Group, 1992.

Peris, Carme & Gloria & Oriol Verges. *The Renaissance: Journey Through History*.
  Barron's, 1988.

Shakespeare, William. *Under the Greenwood Tree*. Stemmer House, 1986.

Stevenson, Robert Louis. *The Black Arrow*. Dell Yearling Classics, 1990.

Williams, Marcia. *Don Quixote*. Candlewick Press, 1993

(Almost all of Shakespeare's plays can be found in print.)

Nonfiction

Ashman, I. *Make This Model Cathedral*. EDC Publishing, 1988.

Byam, Michele. *Arms and Armor*. Alfred A. Knopf, 1988.

Caney, Steve. *Steve Caney's Invention Book*. Workman Publishing, 1985.

Caselli, Giovanni. *The Renaissance and the New World*. Harper and Row, 1986.

Caselli, Giovanni. *The Everyday Life of a Cathedral Builder*. P Bedrick Books, 1992.

Chambelain, E.R. *Everyday Life in Renaissance Times*. Carousel Books, 1965.

Davis, Mary. *Women Who Changed History: Five Famous Queens of Europe*. Lerner, 1975.

Fritz, Jean, and others. *The World in 1492*. Henry Holt and Company, 1992.

Kendrick, Mark and Walter. *The Treasure Book of English Poetry*. Doubleday, 1984.

Macaulay, David. *Cathedral*. Houghton Mifflin, 1981.

Macaulay, David. *Ship*. Houghton Mifflin, 1993.

MacDonald, Fiona. *A Medieval Cathedral*. P. Bedrick Books, 1991.

Millard, Dr. Anne. *Exploration and Discovery From AD 1450 to AD 1750* (Usborne Picture World
  History). Usborne, 1990. (May be ordered from Dale Rettinger & Assoc., P.O. Box 31296, San
  Francisco, CA 94131-0296, Phone 415-285-1175)

Raboff, Ernest. *Leonardo da Vinci*. Harper Collins, 1987.

Venezia, Mike. *Michelangelo*. Children's Press, 1991.

Ventura, Piero. *Michelangelo's World*. Putnam Pub. Group, 1989.

Videos/Movies

There are many videos and movies of Shakespearean plays. Check your libraries and video stores for
appropriate titles.

Computer Programs

Civilization by Microscope, 1991.

The Complete Works of Shakespeare by Reasonable Solutions (Shareware), 1992.

Bibliography *(cont.)*

Teacher Reference

Severy, Merle. *The Renaissance: Maker of Modern Man.* National Geographic Society, 1970

Rabb, Theodore K. *Renaissance Lives: Portraits of an Age.* Pantheon, 1993. A teacher resource that includes sections on Petrarch, Catherine de Medici, Galileo, Gentileschi (a woman artist), and Milton, among others.

Contests

Invent America! is a nationwide program aimed at stimulating K-8 students to think creatively. The United States Patent Model Foundation, a non-profit organization, sponsors a nation-wide contest for young inventors. The Foundation also offers teachers free booklets containing lesson plans, background information and activities for students, administrative ideas for supporting the program, and a resource guide. For these materials, including contest forms, send $1.95 for shipping and handling to:

> *Invent America!—CM*
> United States Patent Model Foundation
> 1331 Pennsylvania Ave., NW
> Suite 903
> Washington, DC 20004.

Music

Instruments of the Middle Ages and Renaissance. David Munrow Angel Records (Capitol) 2 records and 100 page book SBZ - 3810

Seraphim Guide to Renaissance Music. Syntagna Musicum of Amsterdam Seraphim Records 3 records and a booklet SIC - 6052

Lute Songs 1606. John Danyel Consort of Musicke Decca Records London (part of The Florilfgium series) original instruments, details notes, with vocals

English, French and Italian - Madrigals and Songs. RCA Records VICS - 1428

Shakespearean Songs and Consort Music VIC/VICS - 1266

Jackdaws

Jackdaws are portfolios of historical documents. They may be ordered from Jackdaw Publications, P.O. Box 503, Amamwalk, NY 10501-503. Jackdaws appropriate to the Renaissance include:

Columbus and the Age of Explorers

The Black Death

The Spanish Inquisition

Shakespeare's Theater

Elizabeth I

Martin Luther

Answer Key

Page 22

1. 6,048 miles
   3 weeks x 7 days/week = 21 days
   21 days x 24 hours/day = 504 hours
   504 hours x 12 mph = 6,048 miles
2. 550 miles
   Use the mileage key.
3. .8.3 hours
   100 miles / 12 mph = 8.3
4. about 175 miles
   Use the mileage key

Page 25

1. Rudder
2. Mizzenmast
3. Mizzensail
4. Mainsail
5. Mainmast
6. Crow's Nest
7. Foremast
8. Foresail
9. Forecastle
10. Hull

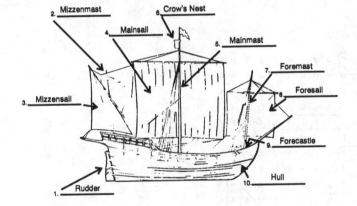

Page 34

1. Shakespeare watched his first play........
2. Shakespeare graduated from Stratford's.......
3. When he was 18 years old........
4. After the births......
5. In 1952, Shakespeare wrote a play......
6. The plague broke out in London ......
7. By 1594, Shakespeare had written five more plays....
8. Southampton paid Shakespeare a lot of money ......
9. In 1599, the building of a new theatre ......
10. After James I became King of England .....
11. When Shakespeare was forty-seven ....
12. After the Globe Theater burned ....

Page 43

1. S
2. T
3. P
4. E
5. R
6. B
7. A
8. I
9. L
10. C

ST PETER'S BASILICA

Page 51

Match these jobs to the pictures.

1. town crier
2. blacksmith
3. cutler
4. peddler
5. minter
6. porter
7. potter
8. puppeteer
9. spinner
10. herbalist
11. poulterer
12. weaver
13. pewterer

Answer Key (cont.)

Page 53

1. tailor
2. brushmaker
3. locksmith
4. fishmonger
5.
6.
7.
8. Answers will vary

Page 56

1. 2 ½" (6.5cm), 3" (7.75cm), ½" (1.25cm)
2. 1 ³/₈" (3.5cm), 1 ¹/₈" (3cm), ²/₈" or ¼" (.5cm)
3. 1 ³/₈" (3.5cm), 1 ¼" (3cm), elbow to fingertip, ¹/₈"" (.5cm)
4. 1 ⁵/₈" (4cm), 1 ½" (3.5cm), knee to toe, ¹/₈" (.5 cm)
5. 6" (15cm), a. ½ b. ⁵/₁₂ (round to ½)
6. a. ¹/₆ b. ¹/₃

Page 58

a. $5 + 6 + 1 \times 3 \div 4 = 9$
b. $7 \times 3 + 4 + 10 \times 2 = 70$
c. $14 + 7 + 63 + 3 + 3 \div 9 = 10$
d. $59 + 2 + 2 \div 9 \times 3 = 21$
e. $42 \times 4 \div 2 + 16 \div 10 = 10$
f. $110 \times 12 \div 10 + 14 - 12 + 10 \div 12 = 12$
g. $13 \times 7 + 19 + 60 - 20 \div 10 = 15$

Page 72

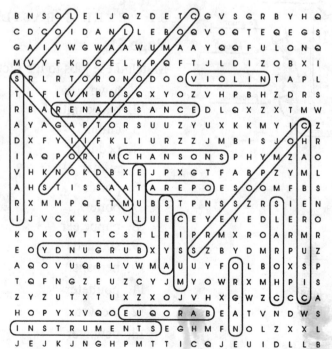